D1743681

Learning

to dance

in the rain

The inspirational biography of a woman's fight to live with a brain tumour, illness and disability

By Anna Gray

5 star - reviews from Amazon, for the first book in the series,

'You are my sunshine.'

'A truly inspirational read, that illustrates a person's suffering, trials and tribulations but still leaves you at the end of the book with a positive outlook on life, and feeling anything is achievable.'

'Very inspirational great reading. Couldn't put the book down.cant wait for the follow up book. Hope Anna is doing good.'

'Inspirational read by Anna. Written with obvious passion for her family and friends who are helping her through her illness. Complete insight to how she is coping with her illness and the accomplishments she has achieved whilst fighting this battle. Remarkable lady!'

'Anna's bravery and determination to beat her condition is inspirational!

As a nurse and a mum I related with everything she said about her experiences and worry for her children! An amazing book and a must read. I will be expecting any student nurse who passes under me to read this and will highly recommend it as it gives all perspectives.

1

God bless Anna and the kids. Hoping for a happy ever after. '

'Loved this book, very well written and I think will help anyone that is struggling with their health and trying to continue their day to day life.'

'An honest and inspiring story that will make you laugh, cry and feel grateful for what you have and who you have around you. This story was a delight and sometimes difficult to read but the positive outlook Anna has on life and the support from all around her is just incredible. Can't wait for the next one.'

Text copyright @ 2017 Anna Gray

ISBN 9781521900215

All rights reserved

Without limiting the rights under copyright reserved above, no part of this publication may be reproduced, stored in or introduced into a retrieval system, or transmitted in any form or by any means (electronic, mechanical, photocopying, recording or otherwise) without the prior written permission of the copyright owner and the publisher of this book.

Dedication

This book is dedicated to all those people who have an 'invisible' illness, who battle on despite great pain and discomfort. I hope that my books can give you a little comfort and hope that life can be better.

In addition, I need to say a huge thank you to all my friends and family, who have loved and supported me with my ongoing journey.

To my fantastic children, Jack and Ella, who have been and remain the best, most treasured thing in my life, love you more xxx

Preface

I thought that I'd give you a quick recap, for everyone who has read 'You are my sunshine', you could skip this bit, for everyone else this is just a very brief recap of 'You are my sunshine.'

You are my sunshine, is the story of my battle with my health and the amazing people around me who helped make my experience more bearable.

In Autumn 2012 - I began experiencing some symptoms which prompted some investigations.

By March 2013 - I was diagnosed with a mass in my brain! There followed lots more tests and a switch of hospitals before I was being set up for an operation.

August 2013 - I was being told that my tumour had 'miraculously' shrank – then came the waiting and lots more tests.

January 2014 - I decided to go back to work – lots of plans and meetings followed and then I went back to work on a phased return. Returning to work didn't quite go as planned; tired, noisy and a difficult colleague!

Then came the Summer holidays 2014 – first of all a lovely chilled week away in the sun, next a fabulous few days in Rome. When I returned I wasn't well; more tests and a stay in hospital, which revealed that my tumour had grown again and this time I had to have surgery.

December 2014 - I had brain surgery to remove as much of the tumour as possible, again things didn't go to plan and I ended up in the high dependency unit, twice; I spent 16 nights in hospital before I was well enough to go home. So that's the story so far!

This is the last chapter of 'You are my sunshine', I thought that it was important to add it again.

Chapter 1

How did I do it?

 In my situation I could have stood back and said,

"Why me?"

But I could easily answer with "Why not me?"

I think everyone has their crosses to bear, their trials to endure and their knocks, so I just felt that this was 'my thing'. Up until this point I felt that I had had a pretty charmed life in many ways, so I knew that I had to take this, I had to find a way through. I have always believed that having a positive viewpoint has helped me and I know that it helps others too; there have been many documented cases where Doctors have been confounded by a patient's recovery when they had been given little chance of survival. To me it gives you a fighting chance, it ups the odds in your favour, it stacks the cards; all the while you feel happier about life in general!

Whenever I am asked if the glass is half empty or half full, I have always been one of the glass half full crowd; I think that I have always thought that way, but that's not the end of the story. I think the other big factor in life is your compassion and empathy, I know that when I was younger mine may have been lacking. I think that life experiences and having children affected me, like many people, I began to question myself more about my feelings and actions. However, the biggest impact was working with children; firstly through foster caring, then working in schools. I challenge anyone to not to realign their empathy when working with vulnerable, hurting children who pull at your heartstrings but who still keep battling away.

How could I say; that my furniture was rubbish when the child that I was working with shares a bed and had to take turns to sleep with 'the' pillow? How could I think that life was cruel to me' when the boy that I was working with had lost his mother to cancer and his dad had rejected him? How could I moan about being overweight, when I had to feed a child before he went home, to ensure that he didn't go hungry? How could I hate my job, when that girl that I was working with told me that I was more important to her that anyone else in her life? It just puts things into perspective, clearer than anything that I have ever experienced in my life.

Over the years I have had to explain depression and it's effects to many students and early on I found that explaining it in the following manner, illustrated it perfectly for them,

'Let me explain about happy juice, inside your body just under your ribs is a place which stores your happy juice; do you recall getting butterflies..... this is happy juice topping up! They will ask is it real, yes of course, most know it's not, but no one to date has argued the point. The fuller the happy juice pot the happier you will feel.

13

When you do good things like; win at football, watch a good film, go on holiday basically anything positive, your happy juice is topped up. Impress the need to recognise all positives, the little ones top up a little but the bigger events top up more but we need all the happy juice we can.

However, when anything bad happens it drains our happy juice; getting a bad result, falling out with friends or having a family member ill. All of these things drain your happy juice.

The next part is important- So what do you think happens when not enough goes in and too much goes out?   They will answer it will be empty.

Right – what do you think happens when it is empty; the answers we're looking for are angry and sad and anything similar, they always know the answer.'

So you can see that I was merely following my own advice! Over time I think that I have trained myself to look for the positives, because I knew that I didn't like my life when I wasn't; in the past I have experienced pain and tragedy, looking back I didn't cope well when those feelings consumed me. I know that personally I have to have a focus, something to look forward to and most of all have people around me who love and care for me; so I make a conscious choice to look for the positives as much as possible.

The more I read, researched and ultimately worked with children on how to help them manage their lives and find ways to be better more positive students; the more I realised that the same resources and notions would work with adults too. If you are preaching a certain way of thinking, on a regular basis you absorb it and take on its teachings too, so in effect I became the product of my own teachings.

Added to all that, I have already said that I like to have things to look forward to, more than that I needed to plan. I like order, I like organisation, it helps me work in the best manner and be more productive; all the way through my illness I had planned my time. Apart from the odd times, even when I was at my worst, I would set my alarm, I would get up and have a little to do list which would vary depending upon my fatigue that day. I would (and still do) only allow myself one PJ day a week, one day to just do nothing and chill out; the other days I had to have 'some purpose'.

I had quickly discovered that I needed a purpose, I couldn't flail about, my Open University studies helped give me my purpose. I wasn't sure of my path, I needed some focus, something to aim for, my degree has been one constant to strive for; but alongside that I had other aims. I wanted to go back to work, or at least be successful in some form of work, I couldn't contemplate a time when I had finished my degree and I wasn't working; I think I would have gone mad. So I began setting myself different targets and goals to achieve, doing so helped me focus on something other than what was actually going on with my health.

Obviously, I had my hurdles and obstacles to get over, but I tried to make them part of my plan, so when something arose, I would think quite rationally about how can I best approach it and get over it and move on. I am not saying that I always did this with military precision and it didn't always work out how I had planned but I still kept trying. Sometimes I did question why me? Surely I've had enough? But these times were few and far between and I think my mindset was quickly reverted back to it's 'positive' setting.

I also felt an obligation to fight my fight and do my best to help myself, there are too many people who lose their battle, I think it is crucial, that those who are given an extra chance at life, as it were, use it well. It is up to those people who are fighting fit to make their lives count, to step up and be the best versions of themselves, they should value their lives and count their lucky stars and never take anything for granted because you just never know what is around the corner for you or your loved ones.

The NHS they had been amazing throughout; I had felt cared for, important and I also knew that my best interests were being considered. I remember when I had first gone into hospital, some 15 years earlier, some of the consultants were brusque and quite frankly rude. However, my experience at the Walton at any rate, had been quite the opposite, they aimed to tell you the truth, to fill in the blanks and to support you in any way they could. I have lost count of how many hospital appointments, tests, scans and doctors I have seen but I thank God every day that we have the NHS which we do. If I had been almost anywhere else in the world, would my operation and everything which followed have been possible? I doubt it, so I will continue to sing the praises of the NHS whenever I can.

I was reminded time after time that my illness and condition didn't just affect me, it was like a stone being dropped; I was the stone and the ripples were the effects on those around me. There were the obvious negative effects; Jack and Ella were made to take on far more than I would have liked, family and friends worrying about me and people just didn't need my grief on top of their own troubles. However, there were positive effects too, one of my close friends has grown greatly in confidence because she feels like 'life is too short' not to, another friend is far less anxious and negative. Finally despite the negative impact on Jack and Ella, it has given them an extra level of confidence and empathy, which I believe has made them even better people than they were before.

Children tend to live for tomorrow and struggle to see past next week, whereas adults tend to plan ahead a little more; some more than others. Despite knowing that I would be limited with what things I would be able to achieve, my 'to do' lists have grown longer and I wanted to do everything as soon as possible. Hopefully, now if I got my pay-out, I would be able to do most of the things on my list. I had always managed to plan in treats for me and the kids using barely any money, just love and imagination but it would make a nice change having more options available. At this point I really didn't know how my life was going to pan out or how long I would have to do the things which I wanted to do, but I was determined to do as much as I could, whenever I could, for as long as I could.

I would advise anyone whether you are fighting a battle of your own, if you know someone who is or if you have as yet been untouched by illness to look at your friends and family and your larger circle of friends and appreciate their value. Often in life we don't appreciate what we have until it is too late and it takes a 'wakeup call' to truly appreciate your life. My advice to each and every one, is not to leave it till it's too late, treasure your friends and family, don't leave it to tell people that you love them, make time for people who you care about; I guarantee that your life will be enriched and happier if you do. People can surprise you in all manner of fantastic ways!

Chapter 2

Hospital to home

On Friday the 19th of December, I was in hospital and I had just been told that if my sodium result came back ok, I could be allowed home; so we waited.......

And waited...........

"Ok, we have your sodium..............." Dramatic pause!!

"Oh come on stop teasing!"

"It's 141!"

"Yyyyeeeeeessssss."

And the nurse said that's exactly what I've just done and we laughed.

"So we just have to get your prescriptions and discharge letter and you are good to go."

We didn't have to wait too long, we had just finished packing up my stuff when my medication arrived. So that was it, I was ready to leave, there was a brief moment of voices shouting in my head, 'OH MY GOD, we're on our own now!!' There was still a niggling little voice saying 'what if; something goes wrong when you get home???' And it scared me, yes there was a hospital 5 minutes away, but it wasn't a specialist Centre.

This is what my discharge letter said,

'Elective admission for EM guided extended transsphenoidal approach and extract craniopharyngioma on 4th December 2014.

- CSF leak intraoperatively, so lumbar drain inserted.
- Admitted to intensive care unit 6th December with high urine output requiring DDAVP.
- Developed hyponatremia due to SIADH and required admission to high dependency unit for hypertonic saline infusion. Endocrinology review advised use of Tolvaptan and fluid restriction which eventually corrected hyponatremia.
- Sodium stable prior to discharge.

Discharge plan;

1. GP to please repeat U&Es early next week.
2. Follow up in clinic with Endocrine team at Royal Liverpool 6-8 weeks
3. Follow up with Mr. Sinha in clinic in 8 weeks with MRI scan
4. Follow up with Dr. Weishman
5. Patient informed to notify concerns.'

     I took an anti-sickness pill, I said my goodbyes to the 'Spa gang', to the nurses and got in a wheelchair; dad pushed me down the corridors and it felt so strange because I had no recollection of going down them over the previous 2 weeks. My life had been the routine and care of the nurses, in the safety of the hospital and now I was going out into the big world and it was scary for me. All I could hear playing over and over again in my mind was being told that,

'Having the surgery won't make you any better, it will make things worse.'

Well I was ready for the fight, I'd come this far being positive and battling and I would tackle whatever was in store for me.........

The journey home wasn't too bad considering that it was a Friday teatime on the M62 and M6, it was weird being in the 'real world'; all flashing lights and noise. I arrived home to a welcoming committee of mum, Jack and Ella, so it was big hugs all round and then I went straight up to my room, I needed to lie down, already. Ella and Jack got my bed sorted into hospital mode for me; my pillows were stacked so high, because in hospital I had had a 'magic' bed and I had slept almost sat up for the whole time I had been there, so we were trying to do the same. They had also brought up some chairs, because we knew that I would have visitors and we needed somewhere for them to sit, we couldn't have them all on my bed like some sort of weird slumber party.

Shortly after I was settled Tes (younger sister), Deb (great friend) and Elaine (45 years a friend!) arrived to see me and catch up face to face on everything which had happened, we were all supplied with brews and so the chatter began in earnest. Ella had kept everyone updated with what was going on, while I was in hospital and unable to do it, but there's no substitute for hearing it from the horse's mouth is there? Elaine also filled us in with what had happened when she had visited, because I had been so confused, I had forgotten most of it. For Deb, it was the first time she had seen me since my operation and she was pretty emotional about it, when she'd heard what had happened in more detail, she was just thankful to see that I was doing alright. We did laugh about my crush on John, the doctor who had come to see me most days!!

It is a weird thing, when you yourself go through some type of trauma, you handle it in your own way but it has a ripple effect upon those around you. It affects everyone who knows you to some extent, some obviously more than others, those closest to you get worrying reports and often feel helpless as to what to do to help. There's another thing too, if a person has been through something similar with another loved one and they lost them, it can make the whole ordeal more real and hard hitting for them. Whatever the reason, everyone reacts in a way that they too can cope with, I was just ever thankful that my closest supports were standing up and helping me through it, despite their own struggles. Having me home would be a mixed blessing for Jack and Ella; on one hand I was home safe and sound, but on the other hand they would have to wait on me, hand and foot!

My next visitor was Charlie, our dog, he was so excited to see me he was trying to kiss me and climbing all over me, bless him. Elaine and her family had had Charlie whilst the kids had been in the travel lodge during my first days in the high dependency unit; he had been utterly spoilt. Elaine's eldest George and his girlfriend, Carla, took him for long walks and Ben played with him and he slept on Maddie's floor, we were so grateful that they loved Charlie as much as we did. Mum and dad were going to stay at Tessa's house because they had been sleeping in my bed and obviously I needed it back. Once we were on our own the kids descended, checking how I was, I asked;

"Are you out tonight?"

Ella "No mum we can't leave you, you've only just come out of hospital."

"No it's not fair on you mum you can barely walk, you might need us." Added Jack.

I was eager for them to go out, they needed the release from all the pressure which they had been under for the past two weeks or so, plus they go out so late that I would be asleep before they left anyway!

"No you must go out, I will be absolutely fine. I will go to sleep and you really don't need to watch me sleep!"

So with some more encouragement, they agreed to go out, I was actually looking forward to a little peace, because I had developed quite a bad head; probably due to all the moving around and excitement of coming home. I got off to sleep ok but I was awake again a couple of hours later, my head still banging and I needed the toilet. I hadn't got my stick, so with my legs still very unsteady and

23

uncoordinated the short journey to the bathroom was somewhat precarious. I lay awake for a good while before I was able to nod off again, but at least I wasn't going to be woken by nurses checking on my vitals and the lights wouldn't be turned on at some ungodly hour either and I was more than happy with that.

I woke in the morning at 8.30, just because I needed the toilet but Ella was up making me a brew, despite having only had a few hours' sleep and feeling a little rough, from the night before. Soon enough Jack was up and we all gathered in my room, catching up on the gossip from their night out, they'd had a great time and I was pleased that they had gone out and enjoyed themselves. I even managed a small bowl of cereal for breakfast, which I actually enjoyed because food had become quite an issue for me; I just didn't want to eat. I was forcing myself to eat in the knowledge that if I didn't, it would delay my recovery, maybe it was being home, whatever it was it was a good turn of events.

Our next task was to get me bathed, in hospital they had a lift type hoist to get you into the bath and a supportive chair to sit on while you were bathed; at home, we had nothing but a chair which sat on the bath but that wouldn't work with Ella bathing me. Jack obviously didn't want to see his mum naked, that would scar him for life; so, it was down to Ella to help me. She managed to help me into the bath, but without the supportive chair it wasn't quite as relaxing as the hospital one. I hunched over as Ella washed my hair for me, despite not having any drips or connections on me, I was covered in bruises and I was still too weak to do it for myself. I managed to give myself a quick wash before Ella helped me out again. It felt like a role reversal, like I was a baby and Ella was the mum, but she stepped up and just got on with it. It took some time to get me dried but Ella was patient and gentle and she got me dressed and sorted into my pyjamas, next she just roughly dried my hair. I felt fresher for it but just like when I was in hospital, I was left feeling sickie and exhausted, so I went back to my bed again for a rest, small steps! I occupied myself with doing some online clothes shopping, I felt like I deserved a treat, plus the kids were going to give me money for Christmas, so I felt justified in spending some money.

Kim (my eldest sister) popped round and helped sort out some bits and bobs for us, next up was Tes and mum; Tes suggested that she could massage my legs for me. I think because I hadn't moved much for the past two weeks or so, my legs were really painful. To be fair I felt pretty fragile; I was covered in bruises and I had puncture marks all over my hands, arms and feet, plus I had my scar on my side, a blocked nose and funny legs!! I felt like I'd been in some sort of accident, I really did look a sight, but I was home and out of hospital and I would have to be patient while I healed. Tes spent a good hour massaging my legs for me, which was heaven, it was so lovely and it did ease my aching legs, for a while at least. Mum had got going in the kitchen and sorted out a meal for us to eat, which was great, she's a fab cook.

Next up on the visiting rota was my cousin Carol, she had been in touch with Ella during the operation and sent food for them while I was in hospital and she came bearing gifts again, one was some ice-cream, because my throat was sore and it helped ease it. She's great company and we spent the best part of two hours chatting away. It had been a mad busy day, so when Carol left I took the opportunity to grab a nap; in the past, I had never been one to take a nap but now I loved a good nap, I needed a nap more often than not. I woke feeling a little better but I was still happy to be in bed being able to just chill and catch up on some TV. Rather than eating what mum had cooked, we saved that and we decided instead to have a Chinese takeaway for tea. I ate the most I had eaten since I had had the operation, which was good, it was tasty which always helps, plus there was plenty left over for Jack to have his fill!

I was still monitoring my fluid in and out, to keep an eye on it, but I was peeing out more than I was drinking, which was odd because I felt thirsty all of the time, so I was drinking a lot. I fell asleep about 8pm, then woke about 9.30 to Ella checking if I had everything I needed, which mainly consisted of cold water for me to drink during the night. I was up again in the night for the toilet and needing a drink, but in between I managed to get some good chunks of sleep in, probably the best I had slept since my operation. On the Sunday I woke feeling a little better again, it was slow progress but at least it was progress. I hadn't anticipated feeling quite that fragile and poorly, I don't know why because I had had major surgery; plus, I had spent most of my time in hospital in the high dependency unit, so it was no surprise really. In hospital, you do nothing and only have visitors for a restricted time, so you are not pushed to do anything, whereas at home you just do more, you see more people and do a little more for yourself.

The one thing which was playing on my mind, was being on my own for any length of time; I couldn't sort myself any food or drink, so I needed to sort a plan of who was going to be with me. Mum and dad were flying back to Spain in a few days time, on Christmas eve, Kim was away visiting them for a week from Boxing day, Tes had plans Christmas eve, the kids were out with their dad Christmas eve because it was his birthday and Ella had booked to go to Dublin for New year, before we knew that I was having the operation. Despite having lots of lovely friends, I didn't want to ask anyone for help over the Christmas period because they all had families and commitments, but I just wasn't sure how I would manage on my own. I did consider consider hiring a 'man about the house' but no one else seemed keen!

My good friend Claire visited and we caught up on everything; she told me about a pilot scheme which she had set up through her job, 'Rally round' it sounded brilliant. Basically it was to help carers caring for loved ones, people who you know will support you, are enrolled in the scheme. When you had a job which you wanted doing; say some shopping or a lift to an appointment, the people who have been enrolled get a notification and whoever can do the task says so. For me it was brilliant, because I hated asking for help and the kids couldn't do everything, so this made it so much easier because you put it out there for everyone; you weren't putting someone on the spot as it were. It was such an awesome idea and it would definitely help me in the weeks to come, it literally couldn't have come at a better time for me.

Another of my friends, Debbie from the Secret Saddo Club (five of us had all worked together and bonded and we still kept in touch and Gemma's son had given us our name) arrived to visit next. She was shocked to hear what had gone on, it's different face to face, more detailed than when you get a short text, I suppose. Again, once she had left I had a nap, it was a good nap too and the beauty of it was I didn't have to move because my bed was my place for the foreseeable future. I cleaned my nose next, using the rinse the hospital had given me, but it really didn't seem to be getting any better; I was still clearing gross gunk from my it, which really wasn't pleasant at all. My nose just felt blocked, like I had the beginnings of a cold, it made breathing more difficult; the rinse was horrid to do and it just didn't seem to be helping either.

Elaine had given me a little book in hospital called 'Hang in there', it's a beautiful book, full of inspirational quotes and it made me cry, I was probably due one and it pushed me over the edge! This is the back page,

'This little book is for those days when life isn't going your way. Its words of encouragement will lift your spirits, help you cope, and remind you that hard times always leave you stronger.'

This is my favourite quote,

'Learn to let go. Refuse negative thoughts and replace them with positive ones. Look for the good things in your life and make a point to appreciate them. Believe in yourself and know that you have the power. You are ultimately the one in charge of your life and the only person in the world who can change it. - Barbara Cage'

I then occupied myself doing an online food order, I had started doing online food orders years before, I had done it then because I hadn't been well either. If you or someone you know is struggling to get out, it is the ideal solution, plus it cuts out those random buys which you often make in store too. Jack peeled the vegetables and Ella made a lovely roast, which was truly the best thing I'd eaten in 3 weeks. The three of us sat in my room eating it because I still wasn't up to venturing much further; it was an odd little set-up but it suited us and I was happy that I was being excused dish washing duties.

The following morning, Monday 22nd, Ella brought me a brew at 7am before she went off back to work after her Christmas break, then I napped again til 9.30 when the nurse arrived to take my blood. Jack sorted me another brew and some crunchy nut cornflakes for breakfast, which were tastier than I expected. Mum and Kim arrived and mum gave me a bath and washed my hair again, I know it's got to be done but it really was a pain in the ass; it was difficult to get done and it left me feeling crappy and irritated afterwards too. I lay on my bed in the dark for a quite a while, my head had begun to hurt again, plus

I had a temperature too, which really wasn't something which I needed on top of everything else. Next to arrive was Tes, she gave me another marvelous massage, it really did ease my aches and pains; I was so grateful that she had suggested it, we did laugh that she had missed her calling. I had yet another nap when everyone had left, because Tor was due and I was exhausted. Recovering was proving to be quite a hard task, to fit in between visits! Tor (my oldest friend from dancing) arrived with Rob (Tor's husband), I filled them in about how things had gone in hospital and how I was feeling, they were full of praise for Jack and Ella and how they had been so good throughout. I was really proud of the pair of them but it meant a lot when other people noticed it too.

Tuesday 23rd, I had another interrupted night's sleep but I knew that I could nap in the day and I didn't have to be anywhere or do anything, which helped me cope. Mum and dad came in the morning for their last visit, before going back to Spain and my aunty Judy and uncle Stuart came to see how I was and to say goodbye to mum and dad too. I hadn't seen them for a while but mum had been keeping them updated and we had spoken on the phone. There were emotional goodbyes when mum and dad left, but I was hoping to go out to see them in Spain in a few weeks as part of my recuperation, if things went to plan. Soon after my friend from my dancing days, Jo arrived unexpectedly and we had a lovely catch up because we hadn't seen each other for a while so there was plenty to chat about. In the evening, Jack was out doing some Christmas shopping and Ella was at work, it was the first time that I had been on my own in the daylight at least and although I was a bit nervous, I knew that I would be fine. I decided to venture downstairs, for the first time because I needed supplies, which probably wasn't the best idea as I was on my own, but I needed a drink. I managed to make a brew and get back upstairs without incident but I was left feeling properly out of sorts, I'd had to rush everything and my body really wasn't up to rushing. I could manage just lying or sitting supported but any sort of moving about and I felt awful, it was improving very slightly, the kids would say;

"Mum you're doing great."

"You have just had brain surgery, you know?!"

"You were in the high dependency unit only a week or so ago!"

"Stop pushing yourself, you've got lots of time, there's no rush."

So I kept telling myself to take it easy, improvements would come but I would needed to take it one step at a time and not rush the process, which was always my tendency!!

Chapter 3

Christmas

I knew that I wouldn't be up to much when I came out of hospital, so I had done my Christmas shopping before I went into hospital, I wasn't normally very organised with buy presents, I tended to leave it till at least November before I even started. We had even put the Christmas decorations up before I had gone into hospital, so that was another job sorted; so when Christmas eve came I was pretty ready; all the presents had been bought and wrapped and as I wasn't doing the cooking, there was no stressing over food either. It had been our turn to go to Tessa's house but we had decided to do it at mine, under the circumstances it seemed like the best choice. I was doing my best to be all festive, by wearing my Christmas jumper, I'd bought new ones for me, Ella and Jack; they had worn theirs to hospital, while I was in the high dependency ward, I wore mine too when I was in my pyjamas and not hooked up to machines.

I had a good start to the day because Jack brought me breakfast in bed which was great, I could've quite easily gotten used to that. Joanna then came, she had been in hospital too so she hadn't been able to come any sooner; so, we swapped war stories and laughed at ourselves because it seemed that neither of us had been particularly good patients! Next to visit was Lyn, my ex mother in law, who had been great looking after my garden when I couldn't do it; she just popped with some gifts for Christmas. She is a former nurse and she popped up to see me and say how lucky I had been to get such first-rate care while I had been at the Walton Centre. Next up was, my friend and former colleague, Tridge, we had son's born on the same day and we were former work colleagues, she's a scream; she has a wicked sense of humour and so she made me laugh.

By the time the kids had gone out with their dad for tea and drinks at 6pm, Carol had arrived and I was already worn out, we had installed a key safe outside so that people could let themselves in and I didn't have to get up and go down, it proved to be a godsend with all the visitors. Carol had brought fish and chips round, oh they were delicious, I love chippy chips, we don't have them often but they really are a treat. So, we both sat there eating them with relish, a little of what you fancy was certainly doing the trick at tempting me to eat. She'd also brought some more ice-cream which was vanilla flavoured Carte d'or, which was delicious, plus it was helping with my sore throat, so it was medicinal too! Carol and I had lost touch a bit, so it was so lovely to have reconnected with her during my illness; every cloud has a silver lining and all that. When I was younger I was convinced that we were actually sisters, because we look so alike and I didn't look like either of my sisters really.

It was like a tag team Tes and her daughter Macy, who had been out for tea with Kim and her boyfriend Ant, arrived just as Carol was getting ready to go, it was perfect timing. We all normally go out for Christmas Eve tea but obviously I wasn't fit for it. Tes began organising for Christmas day and bringing me brews, while me and Macy sat watching

Christmas films which I had recorded. Macy is great company, especially when I am on my own with her, she was just 10 at the time and very much into the whole Christmas experience. We even had a sign out front and reindeer dust everywhere! I was struggling to stay awake but I didn't want to sleep too early and miss all the Christmas spirit, I lasted till about 10pm before I turned off the light, then I just couldn't get to sleep, it's sods law, isn't it? I had a bad head and I felt sick too, so I took some tablets but they didn't help me get off either. I was still awake at 2.40am, every time I was about to nod off, I needed a drink or to go to the toilet; by 4am I'd had enough so I made myself a brew. Next thing Macy was at my door saying,

"Santa's been!!" Holding up her stocking!

"Well he's still not finished, so you better get back to sleep or you won't get any more presents!"

So reluctantly she went back to bed, she still believed and I didn't want it to be me who blew the whistle. Next Ella came to check that I was ok,

"Are you ok mum?"

"Yes, I just can't sleep, thanks."

Then Tes,

"I heard noises are you ok?"

"Yes, thank you, but your daughter has been in saying Santa's been!"

Next up was Jack,

"Is everything alright? Are you ok mum?"

"Yes, son I'm fine."

I think that they had heard noise and just wanted to check what was going on. I ushered them away saying I was fine, I just couldn't flippin sleep! So, they disappeared and I tried to get off to sleep again, still no luck, I kept looking at the clock, thinking 'the kids will be up soon', maybe in hindsight I was excited for Christmas.

Christmas Day 2014, the kids didn't actually get up till 8.30 which was a bonus, me and Tes went down first and she made some brews. Kim and Ant arrived, saying that they had been up ages waiting for our call to come down. Then the kids were allowed downstairs, Macy's pile was enormous, Jack and Ella's not so big but they...........well Jack more, like to have lots of presents to unwrap. Their piles have to have the same number of gifts because the kids take it in turns to unwrap them, plus they have to guess what each present is too, then once they are done, the 'adults' unwrap theirs. I'm not sure when Jack and Ella will migrate to the adult's side, they were 23 and 20 respectively at the time! It took us about two hours for us all to unwrap everything, I do love Christmas but I would honestly be happy if we all agreed on £5 gifts, to me it should be about family and other loved ones; however, I have been out voted on many occasions. Then it was bacon butty time; everyone has their own traditions at Christmas, ours includes a bacon buttie after we have unwrapped all of the presents. Once I had eaten, I went back upstairs to see if I could get in a nap before lunch, but I couldn't get any longer than half an hour before I needed a drink, it was so frustrating. It was like having someone wake you up, just as you were dropping off, but I had no one to shout at because I was the one waking myself up!

Christmas dinner was lovely, small portions for me but I ate it all. We had set up our folding table so we were all squashed round together, it's like what Peter Kay says about Christmas; having odd chairs and people sat at different heights, but that's part of the fun, isn't it? When we had finished eating, Jack and Ella went off to their dads to celebrate it with him, Julie (Mark's wife), Katie (stepsister), and Jake (stepbrother), plus their grandparents would be there too; so, they had a whole other Christmas to celebrate. This is how we've managed Christmas since we split, one year they eat with us, the next they go about 11am and eat with their dad's side. At my end, we sat down and watched a family favourite 'The sound of music', singing along of course, I would love to go to Austria and do the whole 'sound of music experience, I'm sure that it would be fun, expensive, but fun!

I was really grateful that I hadn't had to spend Christmas in the hospital, I was glad to be home amongst everyone I loved. I sent out texts to people wishing them a 'Happy Christmas', I'd really appreciated all their love and support and I told them so. I had been overwhelmed by how many people had wanted to visit me, I had had to have a schedule, so that I didn't get over tired. I even wrote a poem so that people didn't stay too long;

ONE HOUR VISIT

Greetings friends and family,
You are a welcome sight,
But please do be wary,
Cos I'm putting up a fight.

I may look well to you,
But inside here I'm flailing,
My mind is always willing,
But my body is definitely ailing.

I welcome thoughtful guests,
But be mindful when you visit,
As when I entertain too long,
I will always hit my limit.

If you have time to spare,
Feel free to help around,
Cos the kids take over duties,
Once you are homeward bound.

      The main issue that I was having, was my inability to sleep properly; my severe thirst kept waking me up, plus I was struggling to breathe because of my nose and I was still in a degree of pain; consequently, sleeping seemed to be an almost impossible task. At 4 am I was out of drink, so I set off downstairs. My walking seemed a bit better but moving about still made me feel sick and dizzy, so it took a while for me to settle again. Not having a good night's sleep just seems to make everything worse because you just feel tired before you start and all I wanted to do was to sleep in the day, but I knew that would only make sleeping at night even more difficult, it was a vicious circle.

Boxing day, Tes gave me another massage which was just lovely, then Ella and Jack arrived home and Tes left to take Kim to the airport for her flight to Spain to see mum and dad. I felt rotten all day, my legs seemed to be improving but everything else seemed to be getting worse. Despite me doing the rinse for my nose, it was getting harder to breathe it's like I'd got a cold, I was feeling sickie a lot of the time, plus I ached and I was so tired. I was clinging on to the fact that it was a slow process and I was impatient but at least I had no immediate commitments, I could do as I pleased, sleep when I wanted to, so I'd get there eventually; I just had to keep reminding myself of the fact! I had been drinking too much, but no alcohol was involved, and peeing too much and I was worried that my sodium levels would be affected again. So, I sent Mr Sinha, my brain surgeon, an email; I knew that he wouldn't get it straight off, but I sent it anyway!

Dear Mr Sinha,

I am writing with my fluid in and out results for you to peruse, I have been continuing to monitor it closely. Unfortunately, I do seem to have developed a cold and so am suffering with a blocked nose again and a slight temp. I am still continually thirsty and unfortunately for the past few days this has significantly disrupted my sleep, as I am being woken at least every half hour with a great thirst. My fluid levels are quite high, do I need to restrict my fluid intake again? Are my kidneys ok to deal with the volume until I am reviewed in 5/6 weeks-time?

May I also thank you again for all your support whilst I was in hospital It was very much appreciated.

Thanks Anna Gray

Fluid	in	out	Difference	Sodium	/restriction
14th	1200	3710	-2510	127/131	Y
15th	2000	3750	-1570	137	Y
16th	2000	3820	-1820	137	Y
17th	3575	3350	+225	141	N
18th	4450	5600	-1150	139	N
19th Home	4650	4530	+120	141	N
20th	4800	5800	-1000	?	N
21st	5050	4900	+150	?	N

22nd	4525	5120	-495	?	N
23rd	4150	5790	-1640	?	N
24th	4200	6330	-2130	?	N
25th	7350	7600	-350	?	N

The list above is all the fluid in and out from when it was restricted, you can see when I was in hospital, it details the difference and the sodium on each of those days.

Whilst I was in hospital I had moaned about all the checks they did and I was wishing that I could have a check or two to put my mind to rest, typical you always want what you don't have. I now had a herbal diffuser and olbus oil on a tissue in my bedroom to help with my breathing and sleep. Apparently, my room stunk, but I couldn't smell anything, I seemed to have lost my sense of smell since my operation; it proved to be a blessing in that I couldn't smell bad smells and a curse because my taste birds were affected too. The steamer did seem to help because I got chunks of sleep in between waking for a drink or the toilet, so the odd smell obviously worked.

Saturday the 27th and Christmas 2014 was effectively over, but with being in hospital it had been a weird old one for me; I had missed the build-up and all the Christmas music because I had not been out much. On the up side, I had been catching up with friends more often than normal which was definitely a huge bonus. It's so great when someone is struggling for whatever reason, that they have people who care for them, help them out and offer support; I was genuinely amazed at how much people had stepped up for me. I knew that I had a long road ahead with no doubt some bumps along the way and knowing that I had a strong and supportive network was making me feel much better about the prospect.

Chapter 4

New Year

I had decided to telephone the Dot ward at the Walton Centre, where I had had my brain surgery done, just to put my mind to rest about my fluid balance. I thought best be safe than sorry and I knew that it could be days at least before Mr. Sinha actually opened my email. So, I explained what had been happening and the nurse listened and took notes so that she could go and check with a doctor and come back to me with some advice. She called me back,

"Hello Mrs. Gray, I have spoken with the doctors and they have advised that you come in, so that we can take some bloods and get you checked out."

That was NOT the response that I thought I would get, so I was a little thrown.

"Oh right.....eeeerrrrrrrmmmmm........ the thing is, I live an hour or so more from the hospital."

"Can you get someone to bring you?"

"Errrr.......Can I not go to my local hospital? It's just 5 minutes from my house."

"........Just hang on and I will check with the doctors................."

I was beginning to wish that I hadn't called, it seemed like it was going to be more complicated than I had thought.

"Hello Mrs. Gray, the doctors are happy for you to do that, but could you ask the hospital to forward us the results please?"

"Yes, yes of course. Thank you."

So, unfortunately, we had to have a trip to Leighton hospital, poor Jack and Ella were feeling a little dodgy after a big night out but they both came along. Luckily, I was seen by the triage nurse fairly quickly and because my pulse was high and I had a temperature, on top of the fact that I had just had major surgery, I was rushed through and put on a monitoring bay. They took some blood and put in a cannula in case they needed to take more, I was then hooked up to an ECG machine and monitors. They told us that the bloods from Monday had shown that my sodium was 145, which is on the high side of normal; they also told us that the results would take about 1.5 hours, so I sent the kids off to get some food to help them feel a bit better. A lovely nurse took my observations again and when I told her that despite having a temperature I was freezing, she came back with a cup of tea for me, bless. Not too long after, the doctor came with the blood results; my sodium was still 145 which was good that it hadn't gone higher. The doctor said it seemed like I had picked up some sort of virus on top of everything else, typical I never do anything by halves, but there was nothing which they could give me for it. He recommended that I had my bloods more closely monitored and that if I felt any worse I was to go back to the hospital. I was happy that I could go home and more reassured after the blood results were ok. So, we traipsed off back home,

"Mum you really need to just rest up and do nothing, otherwise you're going to take even longer to recover; that's what the doctor said." Ella said.

Jack added, "Stop forcing yourself to do more, it's ok, you've had a rough few weeks."

Again, I was being forced to acknowledge that I was pushing too hard. The kids had set up a little drinks station in my room, so that I didn't have to go downstairs for it. I had a large water container with a tap, with ice and water in, to keep me supplied with ice cold water when I needed it, which was often. They had also set up a small table with a kettle and tea making ingredients so that I could make brews for me and my visitors if needed; I kept the milk in the water container to keep it cold, I must say it was a genius set up!!

"Now you don't have to go downstairs, you've got all your stuff up here."

I was still waking every hour at night but at least now I had supplies to keep me going, rather than having to go downstairs and make myself even dizzier. The following morning Tes came with supplies of extra medication to help with my cold, it cost me £20 but if it worked then it would be money well spent. Me and the kids also freshened up my room; opening the window for a bit of air, to give it a good airing and with any luck get rid of some of the germs too. Tes also did another massage, which she was really quite good at; it did make me feel better, like my own 'Spa at home'. I had yet another rubbish night's sleep and it was really beginning to p*** me off, it was just so frustrating, to be so tired but be unable to sleep; I don't know how insomniacs cope I would be pulling my hair out!

Monday 29th, the district nurse came to take my bloods and she managed it first time which was always a bonus; I explained about the visit to hospital and she was going to follow it up with the doctors for me. I'd decided that I would aim to restrict my fluid intake to no more than 5000, which still seemed a lot but better than the 7500 which it had been in recent days. My blood pressure and pulse were still high and I still had a temperature. It did trouble me, being on the high dependency unit had really shaken me up, more than I had admitted to myself or anyone; being told that I was close to death twice just added to the worry. I was concerned that drinking too much was putting my body under stress and I was concerned about any lasting damage too. I still felt really poorly, I didn't seem to be making much progress and I was beginning to dread going to bed because I couldn't sleep when I did. I just wanted to be on the mend and to me it just seemed to be taking for ever, I was really impatient!

The following day, Macy came around because Tes was off doing some work, she was a star and helped me doing some tidying around; I think that she loved the responsibility and she liked the fact that she was being helpful too. Then my friend and former colleague, Lisa arrived, I'd not seen her, so we had a lot to catch up on; we talked for a good couple of hours, we never run out of things to say, it's a gift! Elaine then called to check up on me and when she went she took Charlie with her, her kids were missing him and he would be treated to lots of walks, while we were busy this end. Not long after I got a call off my GP; he was a bit miffed because he didn't have the information from either The Walton Centre or Leighton hospital; when I was saying about the blood tests he said,

" I shouldn't be relying on you for this information."

At first, I thought he was having a go at me, but he was just frustrated by the situation, about not being kept updated and in the loop, so I understood and it really shouldn't happen that I was telling him rather than him receiving the information from the hospitals. My sodium from my last bloods was 143 and my ATL was a little high, so he suggested having another blood test on the Friday; in the meantime, he was going to review my notes.

'Blood test can measure your liver function and the amount of liver damage. A blood test may be used to measure the levels of the liver enzymes alanine transaminase (**ALT**) and aspartate transferase (AST) in your blood, as these will be raised if you have inflammation of the liver.'

I thought oh no, not something else, but I was still taking a lot of medication, so I thought that it could easily be that. Tes came briefly and rubbed my feet, she had started to do my legs but my legs hurt too much, so she just concentrated on my feet instead, poor girl! Tes likes to be needed, give her a task and she thrives, she gets free stuff all

46

the time because if she's not happy with someone or something, she will say and write to companies and she won't let it go until she is happy with the outcome. She had sorted out a new drier for us because ours had stopped working and got my prescriptions on a scheme so that it saved me money too, bless her. If you mention something to her like 'I fancy that dress' or let's go to London, before you have had time to draw breath, she has it all sorted and booked.

Next to visit was one of my best friends, Joanna, she was feeling a little better and we had a good catch up. I had missed her, because we usually saw each other fairly regularly, however since I had been ill our outings had changed and were now more sedate and low key, which was normally all that I could manage. She filled me in with all of her gossip and night's out, it's good to listen to stories when you are confined to barracks as it were, I was living vicariously through other people, for the time being at any rate. It had been another busy day!!

Then as I was just chilling I got a telephone call off Sheila, my bestie from hospital; my last few days when I was on a normal ward, were made so much better because of Sheila and her humour; we had just hit it off straight away and we bonded through common experience. She was calling to tell me that she had been readmitted to have a blood clot removed and had been really poorly again, she was phoning from hospital but she said that she was due out the following day. It had been another lovely catching up, it's weird how much we have in common and how special she became so quickly, it had really boosted my spirits and hopefully hers too. It also made me think that the little progress that I was

47

making was better than things being that bad that I was readmitted like Sheila.

New Year's Eve 2014 – My good friend Tracey C, who I've known since she was about 16 and she was sneaking into the pub underage, came to see me; we had worked together for a time too, so we knew a lot about each other's lives. We had always met up every few months but with busy lives this had slipped and we hadn't seen each other in probably 18 months, it didn't matter though we still talked for England. She didn't know a lot of what had happened to me and I had missed significant events in her life too. Then another old dancing friend, Alison called for a couple of hours, we had reconnected through a mutual friend, I hadn't seen Alison to talk to properly for about 20 years up until not long before my operation. In our teens, we had spent a lot of time going out in a big group and when we were a little older we had some mad nights out drinking and dancing. We had a good catch up, she had been through some traumas in her life and she talked a lot of sense about trauma and dealing with it all. I think that one of the reasons that pushed me to actually start writing my book was my conversations with Ali, about processing what you've been through in order to heal, I thought that it could help and it surely wouldn't harm.

Mum had flown back here again on her own, to help me out now that most people were back at work; so there were less people around. She arrived about 3pm and did some jobs around the house for me, it was good having someone to help while the kids were at work and she was staying over-night for New Year's too. My next visitors were Lisa (my former colleague and close friend) and Helen, they entertained me for much of the evening, with their stories of Christmas, it was so lovely that they had come around to spend much of their New Year's Eve with me. I was in bed way before midnight, I was happy missing it, I needed my sleep more, but I was still struggling to get a decent night's sleep; I'd tried different things but nothing seemed to help at all, I'd even thought about taking sleeping tablets.

New Year's Day 2015 – I wanted to be upbeat but I was just feeling blahhhhhh! Mum had been up early and Kim turned up and spent a little time with me. I didn't come down until 12ish because I'd had a bath and it still made me feel so rough. Then Carol arrived and took over the baton, while Tes arrived to collect mum. Carol stayed with me for most of the afternoon which was lovely, it was easy and calm. Ella arrived home from her trip to Dublin and distracted me for a while, with all of her stories of her two nights away, it's great that she's such an adventurer; she has said from a young age that she wanted to marry an Irish man, over the years she has added a tall Irish man and if he was a rugby player all the better!

After another rubbish night's sleep, I was still logging my fluid and It seemed that during the day it was fairly even between in and out, maybe a couple of hundred in it but at night I peed at least double and often 3 times as much as I drank. So, I'd been in negative for 11 days which equates to 14 litres!! I just kept thinking, where the hell is that coming from? I know that some comes from what you eat but surely not more than a litre a day? It just didn't make sense to me. I'd also started with a headache and I just didn't feel well at all, I didn't like it, it scared me to be honest. I didn't know if I'd just pushed it too much, or had I had too many visitors, whatever the reason I was feeling really bad. I felt better just lying down doing nothing, but each time I moved I felt decidedly ropey, I felt like I had gone back to how I'd felt when I was still in hospital.

Mum, Macy and Tes came around and then Judy and Stuart called round too, late morning, to see mum as much as me I think. The nurse had been due but when I telephoned them for the second time she said she'd been and got no answer. I was really annoyed because there had been someone there all morning and as I was feeling ropey, I wanted my bloods done, to put my mind at ease. So, I called the doctors about 2 pm, but there were no doctor's available, so I was waiting for them to call back to see what they advised. Nikki's mum Karen, one of Ella's friends was a nurse, and Ella said that I should talk to her; after I told her exactly how I was feeling, she advised me to speak with the doctor and if they didn't get back to me, then I should go to the hospital. I was beginning to feel even worse and more panicky by the minute!

I rang the doctors again at 4.20 and one of the receptionists, who I knew was putting URGENT on one of the Doctor's screen ....waiting. ....4.50 no sign of a call, no call from doctors even after surgery finished. I didn't want to waste anyone's time but I was worried, there was obviously an issue with my fluid, so maybe there was an issue with my sodium, too. So, I left with Ella for Leighton Hospital, it was gone 6 when we booked in with the A&E department. Waiting is not the best when you are feeling rubbish, the seats are uncomfortable and the lights are too bright; plus, there are other sick people too. It is, however, a good place to people watch because there are all sorts of people there.

I wasn't seen until 8 pm, luckily when I was seen I was put through to 'majors' straight away. A lovely doctor took my bloods, I had an ECG and heart monitored, urine test done and the normal general tests and checks. I told them that I should have had my bloods done that day but the nurses had gone away, they didn't seem to mind but I still felt guilty when they came back and said that everything had turned out ok. My sodium was 144, with no signs of organ stress or dehydration, the only blip was that there were some infection markers on the high side, but again they thought that it was down to the virus. All things considered, good news, we were home for 10.30; mind at rest, I felt a bit daft but better safe than sorry. Maybe I was feeling bad because of the virus on top of everything else?

Saturday 3rd and the task of the day was to research ways to get rid of the flu! Also, I hadn't really thought about my Open University studies at all, I was literally on the last stretch of my degree; I just had a few assignments to complete and I would be done. I needed to have a look and see where I was up to and then get in touch with my tutor to see what my options were and how much leeway I could have? What I did know was that I still was no way near ready to start doing some studying. I had no energy or get up and go, it had definitely up and gone and there was no sign of it returning anytime soon. Kim popped for a bit, plus Tes and mum came with some supplies. I then got into a conversation about mum's diabetes, she's type 2 and should be quite strict about her diet so that she reduces the risks to her health. I think because I had little control over my conditions, I got cross with her because she doesn't control her diet as much as she should, she really did very little to help herself with it and in Ella's words I got rowdy!!

I sent another email to my surgeon with an update of my fluids.

Hi again just another update!!

I have been limiting my fluid intake somewhat.

	Fluid in.	Fluid out.	Diff.
29th	4425.	6830.	-2405
30th.	3550.	5230.	-1680
31st.	3675.	4830.	-1155
1st.	3450.	5330.	-1880

This negative output in now 14 litres over 11 days. There have been no positive levels. It can be fairly level during the day but at night it's at least double but often triple what I am drinking. I wake every hour thirsty.

My last sodium on Monday was 143. But the last couple of days I've developed a headache and feel worse than I've felt for several days. I telephoned the Dot Ward, as instructed with concerns, but was told that it was an issue for the doctors and as long as my sodium result was fine there was no need to be concerned.

I am concerned as it is affecting my sleep, and how can I have a urine output of 14 litres greater than input? I would really appreciate an urgent referral to the endocrine team to ascertain what is going on and if need be get treatment.

I look forward to hearing from you,

Kind regards Anna Gray.

I can highly recommend The Walton Centre and I had been so pleased that I had switched from my original hospital but it wasn't easy to just 'pop' in, being a good hour or so away. So, having the facility to contact my surgeon meant that I could keep him updated easily, without any hassle at all. Also, I was lucky because we did have a large hospital literally 5 minutes away, I was always being reminded how good our NHS was in times of crisis. I didn't have to think; does my insurance cover this operation or treatment? We don't realise how good the NHS is until we have to depend on it.

Chapter 5

Visitors and appointments

The following few days continued with the same sort of routine; I would get up and go down for a brew and decide on a course of action. What normally happened was that I would get someone visiting me for a catch up, over the days I had; Kim, Tes, Deb, Babs a great friend from when my kids were young, Tor, Carol, Joanna, Elaine, Claire and Tracey. Once they'd gone I would spend a big chunk of the day chilling and watching TV and normally having a nap. I had my first outing since leaving hospital, one month after my operation, it was the 5th of January and it was my mum's birthday too. Mum hasn't been home for her birthday in about 15 years so we went out for lunch; mum, her three daughters, plus Ella and Jack worked there! Then back at mine, Tessa did my hair for me and she found a small, random bald patch; we didn't know why, we questioned whether it was due to something to do with the operation, but frankly there was no way of telling.

After my emails to Mr. Sinha, my surgeon, he contacted me explaining that he had been in touch with my GP and had asked them to prescribe some medication to help my excessive drinking and passing too much urine. I had been up in the night yet again, thirsty and needing to go to the toilet; it really was causing me some issues, so this was music to my ears. Plus, I was beginning to push myself to get some things sorted, my mind just couldn't rest when I knew things needed sorting; I like lists so that I feel a certain accomplishment when I get to tick things off. It makes me feel so much better when I am on top of things, there was nothing major, I'd made some calls and I had managed to do a little tidying up; mum had been to clean, so I was just rearranging things to how I liked them really. One thing which was really beginning to concern me was that I hadn't even picked up my Open University work, I was still having significant 'foggy brain', I knew that it was useless until my mind was a little clearer.

The hospital had advised that I had more regular blood checks so on the 8th the district nurse had arranged to come; unfortunately, the issues with getting blood were still plaguing me.

- Firstly, when she arrived her box of 'supplies' was locked and she didn't have a key.
- She went back to the office and she returned a little later with the box open. She then failed to get any blood after three attempts and because of this she had used up the bottles she had.
- So off she went again to get some more supplies, when she returned she made several more attempts but she still couldn't get any blood; so, we agreed that rather than continuing to try and running out of options of where to take it from that she would come back again the following day.

"I have put notes on your file now."

"What, about me being an awkward customer?"

She laughed "Well not exactly, just that you have difficult veins!"

That night was the first night that I was taking my new medication 'desmopressin', despite waking up three times, I hadn't needed to get up to go to the toilet; it was progress, especially if it meant that I could have a better night's sleep. Once I started taking my desmopressin, I began sleeping better because I wasn't waking thirsty and I didn't need the toilet either; I still woke up sometimes but not for too long. I was definitely having more good nights than bad night's sleep but I had developed a headache, I had been fairly free of them in hospital, but they did coincide with me being more mobile and trying to do a little more, so I wasn't unduly concerned. I was still feeling sickie and dizzy when I moved around, so one part of me wanted to stay sat still and not move at all but the other half knew that I needed to get moving.

When the nurse returned to try again, she came equipped with lots of supplies. We joked that I was a 'difficult case' and I said,

"I've heard that before!"

"Well, I've certainly drawn the short straw."

Luckily, she did manage to get some blood this time, I was so grateful because I had so many puncture wounds, I looked like a drug addict. Once she'd left I did have a look at my OU studies, part of me just wanted it all over and done with but I consoled myself with the fact that I only had three more assignments to do and I was done and dusted. I had really enjoyed doing the studying and learning new things but

I could have just done without the pressure with everything else going on. I couldn't contemplate giving up on it though, it would just have been a waste of time, effort and commitment, so I just needed to crack on and get it done! I'd begun to try and get myself into more of a routine, the kids were a bit frustrated at me for pushing myself too much, Ella said,

"Mum you have just had a major operation, it's alright if you just chill, for heaven's sake!"

I understood what she was saying, I was saying it to myself but I knew that I liked routine, I felt more in control, I felt more focused, it just suited me, this is what I wrote in my diary,

'Alarm 8.30. Which I really wasn't a fan of to be honest! BUT I need to get into a better, stricter routine, to get myself sorted.'

I was feeling proper fed up, which was one of the main reasons why I felt that I needed to focus myself. There were other things too; I had to have more tests, I was frankly feeling crappy most of the time, my lack of OU work done, thinking about money and then to top it off, I'd gotten a letter about having radiotherapy. So, getting into a routine and accomplishing things would definitely help my mood and give me something more productive to do, so; alarms would be set, to do lists would be made and I would continue to battle on, even if I had to have an afternoon nap every day.

More visitors too; mum was round most days doing bits and bobs, my friend Claire came with her niece Tasha and her baby, Elaine came to catch up and brought her husband Shaun to do a couple of jobs for me, Tracey W called too, Kim popped. Tes was my go to person for getting things sorted like; sorting any issues with my prescriptions, ringing up companies and just organising things for me. Jack and Ella were both working but were great help in between, I encouraged them to spend time with friends because they needed a release from all the pressure they were under; sometimes they would just have friends round rather than go out.

One thing at the top of my to do list was my Open University studies; I began tackling my next assignment, when I had a few hours and I felt up to it, but I was really struggling to stay focussed and concentrate on what I was doing. I hadn't wanted to suspend my studies because of my operation because it would mean that I would have to do my last course all over again and I would have to wait another 6 months or so to do it. However, I was just getting to the point where I wanted to get it out of the way. It had been a good distraction so far, I felt that it could continue to be a distraction and it would be good for me; the trouble was, I hadn't anticipated feeling so rough, so now rather than it being a distraction, it was fast becoming a problem.

On the 14th I was up early and off to Liverpool with Tes for my 'water deprivation test',

'A water deprivation test involves not drinking any liquid for several hours to see how your body responds. If you have diabetes insipidus, you'll continue to pass large amounts of dilute urine, when normally you'd only pass a small amount of concentrated urine. During the test, the amount of urine you produce will be measured. You may also need a blood test to assess the levels of antidiuretic hormone (ADH) in your blood.

After the water deprivation test, you may be given a small dose of AVP, usually as an injection. This will show how your body reacts to the hormone, which helps to identify the type of diabetes insipidus you have. If the dose of AVP stops you producing urine, it's likely your condition is due to a shortage of AVP. If this is the case, you may be diagnosed with cranial diabetes insipidus.'

Now we have done the journey on many occasions but somehow (probably too much talking!) we managed to get off the M6 onto the M62 in the wrong direction, towards Manchester. My sat nav was telling me that we had gone wrong but I ignored that, once we realised, we came off and back on again in the right direction towards Liverpool, but we were very behind schedule. It's one of my pet hates, going wrong, so I was really frustrated because it would mean coming into Liverpool in the rush hour. Then to add to my frustrations I was desperately thirsty but I wasn't allowed to drink and I needed the toilet too. So, by the time I got to ward 9B at the Liverpool Royal hospital, I was desperate to go, the nurses handed me a tiny container to collect my urine in, I looked at it and said,

"That is not going to be big enough....."

She gave me a much larger container which I then nearly filled, as I handed it to her she said,

"Oh right, you did need a bigger one, didn't you?"

The thirst was awful, I wasn't allowed to drink anything and because I normally do drink lots my throat felt like it was bleeding, the roof of my mouth was peeling and so were my lips. Then after about two hours, I was told that I could rinse my mouth but then I had to spit it out, I wasn't allowed to swallow it. Therefore, every 20 minutes or so I would go to the bathroom and rinse my mouth and it felt like torture not being allowed to swallow it. The nurse was also discussing me coming back the next day,

"I was told on the phone that I would be staying here overnight."

"Oh, we don't normally do that."

"The issue is I live quite a way away and so I couldn't get back again tomorrow."

"Ok, leave it with me, I'll talk with the doctors."

The nurse returned with a doctor and told me that due to the volume I had passed they would inject me with the AVP and I would be allowed to drink and eat but they would continue to monitor me. I could have kissed him, but I refrained.

"It doesn't look like we will need you to come back tomorrow, you're results so far point quite clearly to diabetes insipidus."

'Diabetes insipidus is a rare condition where you produce a large amount of urine and often feel thirsty. Diabetes insipidus isn't related to diabetes mellitus (usually just known as diabetes), but it does share some of the same signs and symptoms.

The two main symptoms of diabetes insipidus are:

- extreme thirst (polydipsia)
- passing large amounts of urine, even at night (polyuria)

In very severe cases of diabetes insipidus, up to 20 litres of urine can be passed in a day.

AVP plays a key role in regulating the amount of fluid in the body. It's produced by specialist nerve cells in a part of the brain known as the hypothalamus. AVP passes from the hypothalamus to the pituitary gland where it's stored until needed.'

Normally when I go to the hospital I have a bag of goodies because the shop is so expensive, but because I knew that I couldn't have any this time, I hadn't taken anything with me, so that I wouldn't be tempted. I had to go to the shop and I just got a couple of snacks, plus the nurses brought me sandwiches and water too. Then a man who had been sat next to me all morning, gave me one of his drinks because he had a huge bag of supplies, bless him; he looked like a regular too. The next issue which I had was how I was going to get home; I couldn't ask Tes because she had brought me, Jack and Ella were working and I couldn't ask anyone at such short notice. I went through different options and getting the train seemed the best option; getting the train would mean that I wouldn't have to inconvenience anyone but I hadn't been out on my own and I was still physically weak, but after considering different options it seemed to be my only option. I'd need a taxi down to the station, a train home and then someone would hopefully get me the other end, I had my crutch with me so hopefully I would be alright.

Then Ella text on her lunch asking how things were going, so I explained what had happened and that now I was coming home, but when I said that I was coming on the train she said,

"You can't get the train, that's ridiculous!"

"I will be fine, I can't expect someone to drive up on short notice."

"I will drive up after work."

"No, no I will be ok, it's too much after a long day at work."

"I'm coming, I'll be there as soon as I can."

She wouldn't be swayed and I was relieved to be honest, these tests take it out of you, I'd been up very early and it was only my second venture out. Ella wasn't finishing work until 6 so it would be gone 7 before she was likely to get to me, I would be finished about 6ish, so I would just sit in the cafe until she arrived. In the end Ella's work, La Matternelle a children's nursery, were brilliant and let her go early from work and she arrived just as I was having my last bloods taken about 5.40. We called at KFC on the way back my treat, plus Jack was cooking tea for when we got home too; despite the time we made good time and got home by 7ish.

The following day I got a call from my GP's saying that I now had a water infection and I needed antibiotics. I'd been having pains in my side for a few days but with everything going on I had just put it down to being more mobile, pain was a daily occurrence so I hadn't paid it much attention. I was supposed to take my antibiotics every 8 hours and the daily dose was three but I was only awake for about 12 so I had to alter the timings somewhat to fit them all in. I was feeling pretty rubbish, on top of everything else all the aches and pains, this water infection really wasn't helping me at all. I went up to my bedroom at teatime hoping that resting up would help me some. The day at the hospital had taken it out of me, it had been a long day and I was used to just chilling for most of the day, so I had planned a particularly early night.

I had practically nodded off, when Jack, stood at my door mumbling, you know when you are drowsy and you're not sure what's going on? I woke with a start, stuff like that scares me, I jump at the slightest thing especially when I'm having a sleep, I thought that I was going to have a heart attack! He does it regularly and sometimes he films it because it makes him laugh, the following day I tried to show him how it felt; so, he played me and I played him but all that it did was to give Jack the opportunity to 'play me' with exaggeration and humour!! He is a really good mimic so my plan backfired. I moved all my supplies, which the kids had set up for me in my room because now I was on the desmopressin tablets controlling my fluid, I wasn't as thirsty at night and so I didn't need them, one more step to 'normal'!

Over the next couple of days, I had a few more visitors; Elaine came to see how things were going, Tes came to bring some things and check on me, Joanna called to catch up and so did Lisa too. I went out for lunch with my friend Babs and Tes; it was nice to get out of the house. In between visits, I had had a look at my Facebook pictures and the thing which struck me was that there hadn't been enough 'fun' pictures of me, for a number of years. So, I decided that I needed to make plans to do what I could and record it, even if it didn't involve alcohol; many of my pictures were taken when I had had a drink because it was easier to persuade me to have a picture taken then. I hate having my picture taken but when I have had a drink or two, I don't seem to mind so much! I made a vow to myself that I would make an effort to plan things in, and get out and enjoy life, an excerpt from my diary,

'I'm still here and I need to LIVE a little bit more.'

One thing that I was planning to, was that I was hoping that I would be able to go and visit my parents in Spain. They spend a chunk of our Winter there, I would stay with them and recuperate, have some sun and be pampered, a winner all round.

Since coming out of hospital I had been gaining weight, I wasn't eating big portions and some days I ate very little because my appetite still hadn't come back properly; however, it was perhaps too many goodies from Christmas. I was also still on steroids for the foreseeable future, so that doesn't help issues either. Tes had brought round some clothes that were 'way too big for her', so now I had a uniform of stretchy pants, tops and jumpers. I had never really been a yo yo dieter and my weight had stayed fairly steady, even when I did binge a bit I would eat well and I would be back on track again; I'm not saying that I was the weight I was at 21 but I had it mainly under control. As a result, this rapid weight gain had been a bit of a shock and I really didn't like it, AT ALL!

Chapter 6

Six weeks?!

Whilst I had been in hospital I had written a list of things I wanted to buy and achieve if I got my critical illness payment and one of the top things, was to buy a little motorhome. Despite not having confirmation of a payment, me, Jack and Ella went for a look; it was a very short look because the weather was awful, wintery and cold, so we abandoned the search and went for lunch, instead. The day out had done me some good, I was getting frustrated with my being confined because I was still very much recovering. I was limited to what I could do because I didn't have the stamina to do much anyway but I needed to do something.

On Thursday, the 22nd I had an appointment at the Walton hospital with an oncologist, Dr Husband; he was a lovely doctor, he looked a bit like a mad professor. I had been told, sort of in passing, that I may need radiotherapy but because my focus had been on the operation, I hadn't honestly given it much thought. When I got the letter I just thought, well it's not that big, so surely it won't need much radiotherapy. He started off by asking me questions about the operation and how I was feeling, I think he was just delaying getting to the point really. He began by saying that the tumour was a particularly difficult one, which was why the decision had been made to do the radiotherapy to give me the best prognosis. Then he told me that it would be 6 weeks, Tes and I looked at each other and I said,

"SIX WEEKS?"

"Yes, it will be Monday to Friday for 6 weeks, 30 sessions in all."

'Craniopharyngiomas are histologically benign brain tumours arising from the remnants of Rathke's pouch. Despite their benign appearance, their clinical behaviour is aggressive, causing serious morbidity by damaging the optic chiasm, the pituitary, and hypothalamic area. Currently, craniopharyngioma is treated primarily by transsphenoidal or transcranial surgery, whereas post-surgical radiotherapy is not routinely applied in all patients.'

'Radiosurgery is a way to deliver a single, high dose of radiation therapy to the tumour while sparing other areas of the brain. This technique requires a head frame so doctors know exactly where to deliver the radiation treatment. Short-term side effects from radiation therapy may include fatigue, mild skin reactions, and nausea. These side effects go away soon after treatment is finished. More permanent side effects can include hair loss, learning difficulties, low hormone levels, weight gain, and memory problems.'

I was gobsmacked, I couldn't really take it in; when I got the letter about the radiation I thought well it's not that big so surely it would just need a bit of radio therapy. I'd spoken to friends whose parents had been through radiotherapy and the longest course of treatment had been three weeks, how on earth could I need 6 weeks? Plus, I would be more tired, there would be a journey of an hour or so there and back as well; I actually couldn't imagine feeling more tired but he explained that as the weeks went on it would get worse. Also, he said that it could cause more damage on top of what had already been done by the tumour itself and the operation. In addition, it would delay my recovery too, because I would get worse again before I could really start to recover. All things were going through my mind and as a result I didn't ask any questions really because I was in shock.

Then it hit me, that it would also mean that I couldn't go away and see my mum and dad either, I was just so fed up. I felt that just as I was moving forward to the next stage I was getting pushed back again with yet something else, then just to add insult to injury when I got home, I tried to take 2 paracetamols and choked on them and I was sick in my mouth! EEUUUCCCKKKK! You'd think by then I was used to taking tablets but I was awful at taking them. This is the text which I shared with my closest friends,

'Well here goes with the update!! As my type of tumour can be troublesome, I have to have 6 weeks of radiotherapy Mon to Fri (30 in total) starting in about 3 weeks. After they've done a 'mask' and had MRI and CTs etc!! Only 1% of his patients are people with benign tumours apparently. I will feel MORE tired (if that's possible!) Plus, sickness and hair loss in certain areas. Plus, maybe more damage to the hormones!! So, I can't go away and will feel crappy for a good while yet. Bear with me while I wallow in self-pity a while!!!

I know it could be worse for me but right now I'm feeling proper fed up!! Lol. X

ps. I may well need help with lifts etc!! '

As ever I had the most amazing response, people telling me when they could and couldn't do, days which were best, everyone sent offers of help. There were also lots of 'chin up' type responses, an excerpt from my diary,

'I get that people say 'stay positive, you're strong, you're lucky.....' BUT sometimes I just wanted to curl up in a ball and say NO MORE. It affects everything – holidays, OU, going back to work, just life in general.'

I was struggling to get my mindset sorted out and Ella generously gave up her Friday night plans and stayed in with me; to watch a film and to help to cheer me up. I think that it was worse than when I was told about my tumour because I was in a more vulnerable position. I needed a plan to help get my mood up because I didn't want to be taken over by my dark mood, as a result the following day I decided to share some funny pictures of friends, family and me on Facebook. I sifted through my pictures finding the funniest ones, or those which held special memories, some were embarrassing some were beautiful; each picture had some meaning behind it.

I got lots of lovely comments and it really did cheer me up, it's weird how such little things can help to put you back on track; it's just that sometimes you have to be proactive about it and not wait until it happens. What the Facebook project did was to reconnect me with friends who I'd not really seen for a while, I may have followed their lives on Facebook but I hadn't had that much interaction with them. I had three lovely messages; the first one was off my friend Tracey, we had spent probably 2 years going out and having all sorts of fun before she met her lovely husband, she wrote,

'I have missed talking to u so much, really looking forward to a catch up.'

Then there was my crazy friend Karen, I met her whilst I was working at Shavington, we spent many a Saturday having a drink in the sun or inside when it rained; while her husband was away playing cricket. She wrote,

'I'd forgotten how much of a good time we had.... you've always been such a fabulous and influential friend....'

Then I had a message off Helen, a friend who I have known since school, plus our parents were friends too, I went on holiday with the family when we were young; she also went to dancing, but she's a singer really, an amazing one at that. She wrote,

'God you're amazing going through all this! I'd love to catch up soon.'

So, from feeling proper down the previous day, I was finishing Saturday on a high, I was again reminded how fantastic and supportive people can be, by a simple message or act.

On the Monday, my Aunty Val called round, she isn't actually my aunty but she has been my mum's friend since they were little and she is my god mother as a result. Val is on the wrong side of 70 but she looks and acts so much younger; still goes out partying, she volunteers at St Luke's hospice and has raised thousands of pounds for them. She is so easy to talk to, she has such a great view on life, she just really understood what I was going through and at one point I think I ended up in tears because it was just so comforting. Sometimes you need a time to cry and let it all out, then pick yourself and carry on. She had come at a time when I had had such bad news and she was a tonic.

It was also Ella's day off and she took me for afternoon tea at a local craft village, it was lovely to get out and have a treat. We had a little look around the antiques and vintage sections. I quite fancied a tea set, so that I could have my own afternoon teas; I saw a few but they were quite expensive, I was looking at another and Ella was shouting me over,

"Wait a minute I'm just looking at one."

"No mum come here, there's a great one."

"Give me a minute..."

"Mum..."

"Oh, for goodness sake."

To be fair she had found the perfect one, with 4 little cups and saucers, plus a milk and sugar pot too, we had another look around and I managed to get some plates which weren't the exact same design but which went really well. Ella bought an 80s sequin, sparkly top for herself. The following day, it was a book club night and as I sat there waiting for the girls to arrive; I had a big cardy on, one of my little tea cups and even a cover on my legs; I was the epitome of an old lady!! I looked at myself and said for goodness sake get a grip. When the girls come around we talk about books but also have a good natter and this was the first time that we'd all met up in a little while, so it was nice seeing the girls; Tor, Elaine, Deb and Joanna. It's always a very chilled affair; lots of brews, sometimes cake, lots of gossiping, some serious talk, some moaning but most of all lots of laughs, so it was the perfect pick me up.

I received a letter from Mr Sinha for an appointment on April 22nd, after my treatments so that makes sense but it would be 5 months after my op rather than the 2 that I had expected. I also had an appointment at the doctors for a check-up and I wasn't seeing my normal Doctor, so I thought that I'd have to go through everything and that it would be a pain. However, the opposite was true, she was very thorough and went through everything, asking me lots of questions about what had happened, which was good. Apparently, my bloods were showing that I had yet another infection of some sort but she didn't know what and I didn't have any additional symptoms, in truth it was hard to distinguish what symptoms belonged to what condition or if the medication was causing further problems. In the end, she gave me another cause of anti-biotics to take which would address whatever it was.

I was so tired that I was up in my room and ready for bed by 8pm, it was like groundhog day; I slept so much and then while I was awake there was a little activity each day and the rest was 'just chilling'. I wrote this in my diary,

'I keep thinking that if I ever wrote a book my life isn't interesting enough; in one sense, extraordinary but day to day, damn ordinary!!'

I'd read in a letter which I had received from the doctors, which said that my tumour was a 'grade 1 craniopharyngioma', so I looked up what this meant and from what I gathered; 0 is no impact on surrounding structures, 1 was displacement and 2 was invasive. I knew this because it had been explained to me many times that the tumour had cause a significant degree of damage, because basically where it was there was no room for it to be. While I was there searching, I did a little more 'Googling', up until this point I had always been happy with my searches; I had been more well informed as a result and I had just felt more in control and knowledgeable about what was going on, however this time was different. To put it in a nutshell it's a slippery little bugger and reading what I found did make me go 'Oh shit!!!!!!' Mentioning morbidity rates and 70% chance of regrowth and success of second surgeries being limited. Here are some bits which came up,

'Total resection may be attempted, but radical surgery can have as high a mortality rate as 10%, and a high severe morbidity rate. Maximal safe resection followed by irradiation is the currently accepted modality of management.'

'Tumour responds slowly to radiation, and in some patients, radiation induced oedema can worsen the symptoms. According to the literature complete tumour removal by radical surgery can be achieved in 18–84% of selected childhood and adult cases. Aggressive surgery with gross total resection (GTR) of the tumour, however, may result in significant and devastating peri- and postoperative morbidity especially after resection of tumours invading the hypothalamus.'

'...Significantly lower than in patients with subtotal or partial tumour resection in whom tumour recurrence occurs in 25–100% of the patients. In these patients, adjuvant radio therapy significantly improves the tumour control rates with recurrence rates ranging from 10 to 63% at 10-years follow-up. Thus, patients with subtotal resection without subsequent RT have the highest risk of relapse.'

Not the best reading and that's just a small selection of what was out there! It was the first time that I had been properly freaked out due to what I had read. What I was thinking was that my tumour was still there, they hadn't been able to remove all of the tumour due to the risk of damaging my hypothalamus further because damaging it beyond repair could be fatal. Looking at the information it was vital that I had the radiotherapy to give me the best chance, but what were the odds for me? I'd never asked about my prognosis and statistics and that was probably for the best, I'm not sure that I wanted to know; but one thing I did know was that as I would be doing as much as I could for as long as I could. What it did make me think was that I needed to do the travelling I wanted to do and not leave it till 'later'. There was so much to organise beforehand; how would I earn money, work on the house I wanted doing, buying a motorhome. Lots needed organising but I was now, more than ever, determined to get it done.

I was getting some things sorted but I was still getting frustrated that I couldn't get what I used to get done, I was literally running on empty all of the time, so I had to plan my day accordingly. One thing which I had planned was an afternoon tea for my 'old' friends; Elaine, Tor, Deb, big Jo, little Jo and Tes. Big Jo, is tall and another old dancing friend, plus she used to live down the road from me too and little Jo is small, and she again is one of my old dancing friends. Tes had come a couple of days before and made cakes for the occasion, under my guidance and instruction and I was able to use my new tea set too. We (by we, I mean Tes) had made cute little sandwiches the crusts cut off, then there was a vast array of cakes and some fruit too; it was a lovely afternoon. There was lots of reminiscing, lots of laughter, some tears and lots of noise! Beforehand I had said that there would be a cut off, because I knew what happened when we got together nattering, it could have gone on for hours and hours and I would have struggled. I had said that it would finish about 6pm, in the end it was a little after at 6.45 and I was in my bedroom by 7. I was exhausted, it would be so easy to not 'do' things, just chill at home and conserve my energy, but what life is that? Plus, you would surely have so few positives to focus upon, it's like you are waiting for some sort of miracle; my advice is to get out and live a while, until the miracle comes.

On the 3rd of February, I had a call off Ruth, a receptionist at the doctor's surgery, she was chasing up appointments for me, it's normally something that I have to do, so I was so glad that someone else was taking the reins. The endocrine (hormone) tests which were booked for the middle of February needed to be put back until after a month after the radiotherapy because the radiotherapy could cause yet more damage and that would need to be taken into account. First it was the tumour, then the operation and now the radiation was going to add to it all damage and mayhem! So, this would also mean pushing back my appointment with Mr Sinha because it was pointless seeing him without any results from the endocrine team.

In other news, I'd also received a letter from Aviva, the company who was handling my critical illness claim; I was somewhat nervous in case it was bad news but when I called them it was to get bank details 'just in case'. It didn't say whether I was or wasn't getting the money or indeed mention anything at all about my claim. Back on the 21st of January I had sent an email, saying to expect a letter,

'Dear all - copy to Mr A. J. Sinha, Professor Vora and Dr Neary

(Mr Sinha please could you forward Prof Vora a copy)

I am writing to forewarn you that my insurance company may well contact you; I have a 'Critical illness' policy, which I am keeping my fingers crossed covers me for my tumour.

The following is the wording from the said policy –

Benign brain tumour - The definition in your policy document:

A non-malignant tumour in the brain resulting in permanent deficit to the neurological system. Tumours or lesions in the pituitary gland are not covered.

We also cover benign intracranial tumours which have required surgical removal, excluding cysts, malformations in the arteries or veins of the brain, haematomas and tumours in the pituitary gland.

This means - A non-malignant abnormal growth of tissue which can lead to a life- threatening situation due to pressure on areas of the brain. The excluding conditions are typically non-life threatening.

Looking at these definitions I think I'm covered!? I am sorry for any inconvenience caused by this,

Kind regards and thank you in advance, Anna Gray'

So I was just waiting to hear……..

Chapter 7

The Clatterbridge

Thursday 6th February was my first appointment at the Clatterbridge Hospital, on the Wirral; it's a sprawling hospital with mainly old buildings and some new, the cancer centre, where I had to go, was one of the new buildings. It was clearly sign posted and it was right at the end of the road, there was a man checking as you went in, he checked my letter, the car park wasn't big but at least it was we didn't have to pay to park. Tessa had driven me and we went in and to the reception, one of them then showed us along and around and down and up a maze of corridors to a room where we were asked to sit and someone would come to me.

First thing I had to have done was the mask, the nurses came in and explained what would happen in detail before they did anything. They explained that the mask was basically a sheet of soft mesh type plastic, it was kept in a warm vat to keep it pliable until it was fitted.

'Thermoplastic mask:

This mask starts as a flat sheet of plastic attached to a frame; it is placed in a hot water bath where it becomes soft and flexible. It is then placed over your face and neck and feels like a warm, wet flannel. We mould the plastic sheet to your shape, which can feel a little strange but is painless. The mask sets in approximately five minutes and is ready to use straight away. The mask is perforated therefore allowing normal breathing.'

What surprised me was the size of the mask, it didn't just cover my face but my neck and all the way down to the bed that I was lying on. It was hot first of all and the only panicky bit was when they put it on first on, you can't breathe until they pinch the nose section up a bit, so you can breathe but it is still weird. I had to continue to lay still for a few minutes while the plastic cooled and set in place, if I moved the mask wouldn't fit snuggly enough and the radiation beams wouldn't target the correct place. I'd had lots of pictures taken whilst I was in hospital so that they would serve as a reminder to me, so Tessa took some pictures of me.

Then I had a CT scan done with the mask on, I was clamped down in it so that my head couldn't move; again, not the best feeling but you just have to suck it up and get on with it. Next was the MRI, now normally I'm not a fan but this time I did have to battle harder than normal to convince my mind that I was ok, so that I didn't freak out. I wanted to pick up any relevant information to help me, the trouble is it's a cancer hospital and I'd not got cancer; I was one of only 1% who attended the hospital but who didn't have cancer. They have a large MacMillan help centre there; I picked out some booklets from there about making plans and taking control as these were sections which I knew would be useful.

Then the worst part – I HAD TO BE WEIGHED – I had been feeling fat, I'd questioned was it the steroids, was it me not eating right or was it just one of those things? I was 74kg in hospital, 79kg a few weeks later and today 83Kg!!! I had put on 9 Kg in 6 weeks, bloody hell I literally felt like I was putting on weight every day. I felt so fat, my weight had always been fairly steady; I'd put weight on gradually over the years but not like this. I had been thinking that I needed to eat ultra-healthy, we didn't eat lots of rubbish as a family but now I was going to restrict my food and see if it's me or the steroids. I'd decided to cut my hydrocortisone down to 15mg a day from 20 mg, I think what had freaked me out, was when I was in Liverpool having tests, a man sat next to me had put on 5 stone, due to steroids!! I let Mr Sinha know, but he said that I wasn't allowed to reduce it any further.

My first night out where I had to dress up as it were, was for my friend Babs' birthday, along with Tes and Joanna, we went to a local restaurant, early doors. Residence is a lovely, plush place and we had some gorgeous food and entertaining chatter. At one point, we were talking about the 'Undateables' show from Channel 4 and Babs said,

"You could go on that."

We all just looked at her and laughed,

"Thanks Babs, am I now an undateable?"

"No, you could be the other person."

"Oh, now I can only date an undateable?" By this point we were all just howling.

"No, I didn't mean it like that.........your situation is.........complicated, and that's the sort of people they have on there!"

I got what she meant, kind of, I wasn't in an ideal position to attract someone, especially at the moment because I had so much going on; it would be unfair to someone to expect them to take it all on board, so it will be just me for the foreseeable future at least. Going on a date, 'undateable' or otherwise was so far from my agenda, I could barely get myself sorted never mind contend with someone else.

Next, I showed them the pictures which Tes had taken of me in my mask, Joanna exclaimed,

"Oh god, you look like a turkey!"

And we were off again.

The following day Tes and I had gone to town to get lots of supplies of fresh fruit and vegetables for my health kick, we went in a local café for a break. Me and Tes were getting on better than we had done in years and we were enjoying our drinks when Jack appeared in front of us;

"I'm just going, I'll be back."

We sat there for about half an hour, but he didn't return; then we began thinking, how did he know we were there, because we hadn't told him? He wasn't answering his phone either to ask, so we sat playing different scenarios of how he could have known we were there; did he see us through the window, did he hear us, did someone tell him we were there, did he have a tracker on my phone? When we did finally manage to catch up with him, it turned out that Jack and his girlfriend were sat opposite us, having a 'talk', and we just hadn't seen them or even considered that option. It was so obvious we had missed it!

I spent the next few days in a similar routine, struggling to get up, then setting myself some tasks to complete so that I didn't feel like I was wasting my days. I tackled some more of my OU project which was going ok, but I was eager to get my studies finished; I'd been doing my studies on top of my job and everything else going on in my life, for the previous 4 years and I was running out of enthusiasm and drive. I wasn't regretting that I had done it, I was just wishing that I had finished it already, my pride wouldn't just let me do 'just enough' because my scores had been good, I didn't want to let myself down at the last hurdle.

I read through all the information which I had collected from the Macmillan Centre and it prompted me to also do some research on any help and benefits which I might be able to claim. Feeling as I did I wasn't sure when or if I could return to work; working full time in a school was pretty full on even with the less demanding role I had been given. At this point the thought of returning to work was stressing me out, but what would I live on, my sick pay was about to end and I didn't know what options were available to me and looking on the internet didn't make it that much clearer. I needed a clearer picture of what my options were.

On Friday 13th!! I was back off to the Clatterbridge, for an appointment with Dr Husband again, this time Kim took me; she doesn't really like the fast roads but she did really well, it's not the best route for those who don't like fast roads, M6, M62 and 57. We arrived early but we were told that the doctor was running late and the nurse advised us to go and get a drink. We were seen nearly an hour late, Dr. Husband explained how the radiation would work and how it would all go; he also explained that with cancer the radiotherapy had an immediate effect but with benign tumours they could often swell but then reduce over months or years even. We literally saw him for about 2 minutes, I managed to ask,

"Are you always this late?"

"Yes, he is." Replied the nurse.

"Oh gosh really?"

We laughed and said our good-byes, but I was left thinking I have to see him every Friday for him to check on how things were going; I would have to bring something to occupy my time next time I saw him.

On the Saturday, it was Valentine's day! I was off to the pictures with Joanna, to see 'Fifty shades of grey'; we'd read the book for book club but there was a mixed response to it. We liked the film and for those who haven't read the book, the books are more graphic than the film! Then on the Sunday, I was out for tea with the Secret Saddo Club (my old work colleagues), all members were there which made a pleasant change; Claire, Gemma, Deb and Emma plus Emma's husband and son Andrew too. Emma lives down south so getting us all together was a bit of a logistical nightmare.

I had spoken to a group of my friends about whether they would be able to be on my 'lift rota', when it would suit them to take me so that I could begin to arrange lifts to take me to the Clatterbridge. I was still waiting for my start day and the times when I had to go, I reckoned that I had enough people to cover all of the 30 sessions, but I would need the dates to be sure. My first day scheduled for radiation was Wednesday 18th February, my friend Tracey W, had a day off work to take me bless her and because it was the first session, we had more waiting around while my schedule was sorted. We sat in a big waiting room with little seating areas, there were two reception desks, a tea and coffee station and a hand massage area! When I was called I went to sit outside of the room and a nurse came and took me in, it was a large, well lit room with a huge machine in the centre and another inner room where the nurses went while the radiation was being administered. I didn't have to get into a hospital gown, I just had to take off any thick layers like jackets and jumpers.

I lay down on the scan bed as instructed and they placed the mask over my face and clipped it into place, then they went into the other room. The mask was on longer than I had anticipated and I literally couldn't move my head at all, plus my nose was still pretty bunged up so breathing was a bit of an issue too. I'd given my nose a good blow but it was still bunged up somewhat, it just didn't seem to be clearing up. The first session over and it was ok, not my favourite thing but in the grand scheme of things, it was bearable.

I'd been given my schedule for the next 6 weeks, so when I got home, I pencilled in who I thought could give lifts on particular days and contacted them to confirm that they could. Ella wanted to do it on her day off, my friends who worked in schools were restricted to the holidays and friends with children struggled if the appointments clashed with school times. When I'd done and got back everyone's responses I was only left with a few that I didn't have covered, so there was just a handful which I needed to organise. I also wanted to have people on back up, so that if anyone couldn't do their allotted days I could get it covered. I felt pretty confident that I would have it covered; thanks once again to my amazing family and friends.

On the Thursday 19th - Lisa, one of my teacher friends took me; I really didn't like how it held my head it hurt. Friday 20th - Joanna, another of my good teacher friends took me, as well as the radiation they took a CT scan too, so I was clamped in the mask for another 10 mins which was awful. I had to do what I did when I had an MRI, I had to lie there and imagine that I was somewhere else, like a gorgeous beach.

I'd decided that during my 6 weeks of radiation I would plan in something good to do at each weekend, so that it wasn't all just about the treatment. I knew that I would be tired but I thought I can sleep on the weekdays and on the 'other' day at the weekend, I felt like the positives which I would get from some treats at weekend far outweighed any negatives. I gathered together some ideas for what I could do and contacted different people so I was spreading myself about as it were and I managed to get all the weekends covered with great things which I could look forward to, if I felt down during the week.

The first weekend, Ella had a won a one-day spa pass for two people and I convinced her that I was most in need. It was at a wonderful 5* hotel, Rookery Hall; Posh and Becks got engaged there! I was feeling frumpy and old and it didn't help having to tick the 46-55 box on the registration form, I skirted over the operation, somewhat so that I could get my massage done without questions; back neck and shoulder it was lovely and relaxing. Then we met in the RELAXATION room which was heaven, cosy beds with blankets and everything, with relaxing music playing, I could have lain there all day. Next, we tried out their steam room but we only lasted 5 minutes; the hydrotherapy pool was more to our liking. It was a relaxing few hours and I was grateful that Ella had taken me; we finished off the day by going out for a late lunch at one of Ella's favourite restaurants The Bickerton poacher, gorgeous food; Jack had come along too because he rarely says no when there is food involved!

On the Monday 23rd - Babs took me for my treatment, the journey was a pain a good hour plus on the way there and a good hour and a half on the way back but she has a fab car so at least it was in comfort. The other good thing about the journey, was that it meant that I could catch up with whoever was taking me.

On the Tuesday, I had to be up for a phone call from Occupational health – going back to work this time was going to be a more complicated process because of the operation and everything since; so, I would have to jump through lots more hoops to be able to get back to work this time. It seems ridiculous in the circumstances that I was even thinking about going back to work but my money was stopping and I didn't know if I was getting any from my claim, my thought was that it was better to go back during the last few weeks of the term, than to go back in September when the pace was definitely more manic. I think I just needed to know if I could do it, to test myself as it were, at this point though I kept my plans quiet, for fear of a backlash from the kids especially. Later in the day Tes took me for my treatment and there were no issues, no drama; just a chunk out of my day!

Wednesday - mum and dad facetimed saying that they had booked their ferry and they would be back on the 27th of March, just before I finished my treatment. It was Ella's turn to take me, so she suggested that we stop at a shopping village on the way for food, just to make the experience a little more pleasant and then we went onto the hospital for my treatment. Not long after I arrived home, Carol stopped by with a lasagne for our tea and she stayed for a catch up which was nice.

On the Thursday – Tridge (my friend from work) took me, she was having a tough time herself, her dad had been poorly and he lived away so she was wearing herself out going back and forth to help take care of him. It must be awful to have parents living away from you, when they are ill and you needed to be in two places at once. So, the journey was good for talking about it all; it doesn't matter how you are doing in your life, there will always be other people who are struggling with some aspect of their life too, I just hoped that in talking to me about it all it had helped a little bit.

Friday – was a longer session because I had my treatment, a CT and then I had wait to see Dr. Husband after wards, Kim was taking me and so we went prepared with packed lunches to eat while we waited. I had to fill in a questionnaire with a nurse and after she read it, she said that she would assign me a specialist nurse for added support and information, I'd been offered this on a couple of occasions before but the help had never materialised, so I was keeping my fingers crossed this time it actually happened. Just before my appointment with the Doctor, I had to be weighed again, 85 kg, more again and I'd been cutting down too!!! The doctor asked how I was doing and I told him that I seemed to be peeing more at night time, so he suggested taking a full tablet at night rather than a half tablet to see how I went. I hate that I had to take so many tablets but if it meant that I could sleep more and keep my fluid balanced then I was willing to give it a try.

The second weekend I was having afternoon tea again, this time at a local restaurant and bar The Cat, I went this time with my friend Lisa and it was absolutely delicious. The cakes especially were amazing, there was this gorgeous fruit cake and the most delicious brownie. Really after my weigh in I should have been having salad and water but I told myself that it was 'happy' food and I needed it. It was nice to be out and have a fun afternoon but I was so tired that I spent most of the rest of the weekend in bed; but I could deal with that, knowing that I had been out in the week and I had been out at the weekend too. A little balance in life is what it's all about; all hospital and no play would make me a very unhappy lady!!

Chapter 8

The CALL!

On the Monday Ella took me again and we stopped off at a wonderful local ice cream place called 'Snugbury's' before we travelled on to the Clatterbridge. A nurse spoke with me and she said because my fluid balance seemed to all over the place, I would need some blood tests to check on my levels, so she arranged for me to have them taken the following day. Jack took me the following day and I had my bloods taken before my treatment, however when we booked in, the receptionist told us that all six scanners had had issues and were now running about an hour behind. To be fair it was the first time, they normally ran well and on time, so because Jack was with me and we would have to wait longer than anticipated, he needed refuelling, so we nipped to the café; but in the end, I was in only about half an hour late.

On Wednesday the 4th, one of my oldest friends Tor took me, she's ace but she doesn't like the fast roads so we went at steadier pace but we arrived in plenty of time. The mask felt really tight for some reason, most days it only lasts a few minutes but it is a lllooooooonnnnnnnggggggg few, when it is so tight and I am struggling to breathe. Plus, to add insult to injury I had begun to feel really sickie and I'd got a bad head to boot, I must have been having a bad day because this is what I wrote in my diary,

'My overwhelming feeling the more I think about it is, that by the time this is all done and dusted I will have 'missed' out 3 years of my life!! I'm now old!'

The next day Elaine took me, she's like the voice of reason, it's weird how my friends are all so different and great that they all offer me something different. Maybe that's why we chose who we do, to be part of our lives, because they bring something which we need and vice versa too probably.

I read something on a brain tumours in a leaflet which I picked up from the Macmillan centre in the hospital. Then later I looked at more information online about craniopharyngiomas and as per usual of late, I found something else that freaked me out; they CAN turn malignant and then the prognosis really isn't good. I think that I could remain so positive and upbeat because I knew how lucky I was, I don't think that I comprehended how much until after the operation and everything which had happened in hospital. As I didn't want to admit to myself how big a thing it was, because I had no choice, it had to be done. I thought that I'd had my bad karma but now it just seemed to be one bit of bad news after the other, however, I'm not sure I'd cope if I was told I that was going to die soon, I had trouble even saying it.

On the Friday, Tes took me; I had my treatment which is always longer on a Friday because they do a CT too. I suppose a CT is needed for the vast majority of patients who have cancer and whose CTs are done to show whether the tumour is shrinking or not, but for me it seemed a bit pointless. We had lunch in the café before my appointment with the Doctor, we were in there about a minute because things were progressing as they should have been and I didn't need to discuss anything with him. Oh, and I had to be weighed again, and again I weighed more, 86kg!!! I even wore lightweight clothing and I'd cut down, dear lord I'd explode if this carried on and I'd have to live in stretchy pants for the rest of my life. I'd end up one of those people who ends up being cut out of their house because they couldn't get through the door!

Focus on the good, focus on the good! As I've explained before I had planned something to look forward to each weekend to make the treatment more bearable and this weekend was no different. Tes, Elaine and myself were going to watch a production of the musical 'Joseph and his technicoloured dream coat', it was brilliant. I had seen it a few times before but I really like it; the songs are catchy, there's humour and it's a great story, what more could you want? As an added treat, we even had ice creams at the interval. Then in the evening Joanna came around and we watched a film together and had a good old natter, which finished off a great day. On the Sunday, I just had a lovely lazy, chilled day with the kids sorting out a roast dinner; it had been a pretty perfect weekend all round, just what I had hoped for.

My aunty Val popped in the following morning, before we went off to the hospital, she's a breath of fresh air. She brought flowers and apologised again that she couldn't take me, she doesn't like driving that far, I assured her that I had enough people who could, so it was no bother at all. She'd brought some literature and some photos from her cruise, she has been on lots of cruises, all P & O and so she was telling me all about it all. It just made me want to go out and book one straight away, but I couldn't without the money.

All three of us went off to the hospital; me, Jack and Ella, everything went well with my treatment, no issues, no problems. Then on our way out we called in the shop for some supplies; Jack had lagged behind and hadn't seen us go into the shop. He carried on walking and walked outside and we could see him looking around bewildered, trying to find us, it was most entertaining. Eventually he went towards the car, still looking around frantically for us and when he got to the car and we weren't there, he just began shaking his head! By the time we went outside he had walked back towards the entrance,

"Where have you pair been?"

"We've been to the shop."

And with that he was distracted because he saw our supplies and as ever he was 'hungry'.

The following morning, I woke and I just couldn't get myself going, every part of my body hurt; was it because I was inactive, effects of the medications I was taking, just getting old or something else? I felt that bad that I even had a little cry to myself before Deb arrived to take me for my treatment, which was a real rarity for me. She was struggling with a death in her family and she just needed to talk it through and I was happy to talk and be there for her. We all need reminding that there are lots of other people struggling on a daily basis, it made me think about my situation again. Tes took me again the following day, no problems or issues.

On Thursday the 12th, I had struggled to get anyone to take me, some people I didn't want to ask again because they had already taken me and others just couldn't take me. So, I had to call on one of my back-ups, so my ex-husband was taking me, strange but true. He had been on my back up list, if desperate, a list of people to call and today was one of those days. I had been feeling really sick and my one worry was that I might throw up in his flashy car! Despite what the kids thought, it wasn't awkward, it was fine. He had taken a different route there, more windy roads but it was actually a nice change, it wasn't until we were almost back that he said that his car had different comfort settings,

"What's it on now?

"Sport."

"Haven't you got a comfort setting?"

"Err....yeah..."

"Well wouldn't that have been the best setting for me?"

Muppet!! But it was good of him to put himself out for me, so I really couldn't complain.

Friday's shift was Kim's, treatment went well and then came the weighing........ 84kg so better than last time, so all the sickiness did have a positive side at least. For some reason, I had a ridiculously red face and Kim said I looked like Aunt Sally and I thought that I looked more like one of the Diddy men! We waited ages again to see the doctor because I needed to speak with him about the issues that I was having with my nose; it was constantly blocked and painful, plus I was still getting horrible gunk from it too. He explained that after the type of surgery which I had had, it could take a long time to clear up; so, he prescribed a nasal spray which turned out to be worse that the nasal rinse which I had to do.

On the Saturday, my lovely friends from hospital were coming, Susie and Sheila, so first thing I had a shower and I thought more hair than normal had come out and when I brushed my hair back there was a bald patch! To me it looked huge but it was, in fact, about the size of a golf ball right in the middle of my fringe, I looked at it and just cried. I knew that there was a possibility that I was going to lose some hair but I had imagined that it would be at the back where I wouldn't see it!! I looked at myself and literally said out loud,

'It is a small patch, lots of people have it worse, so get yourself together and get dressed!"

I managed to clip the rest of my fringe across to cover the bald patch but I was very conscious of it. Sheila drove and the girls arrived and there were big hugs all round. We had such a lovely catch up because we had all been through similar things, we understood how the others were thinking and feeling. We all talked about how we were feeling and what things we were struggling with on the whole, we had a moan in private but tried to live our lives in public as positively as possible. There's so many things in life which we can't control but how we deal with a situation is in our control and we can make a positive or a negative choice.

Mother's Day, Ella had bought me a beautiful scrap book with bits and bobs stuck in, it was to record all of my travels in; she had gone to her room several times over the previous week or so and she never did that, but she had been doing my scrap book. Jack, after being prompted by Ella, had bought me a foot massager and flowers, which was lovely even if had been a little last minute. Tes came around and checked my head and thought that it was just the front bit which was a relief. Then Tes, Macy, Me, Jack and Ella all went out for a beautiful roast lunch at the Bickerton Poacher, it was nice going out altogether, there was more people to take the mickey out of. We then decided to go onto the ice-cream farm for some pudding, there's was so much choice, it took a while for us all to choose and it was heaving with people having ice-cream despite the cold day.

Then the next morning I had THE CALL, it was surreal, it went something like this,

"Hello is that Mrs Gray?"

"Hello."

He then went through a few security questions,

"This is Axa Insurance, I am ringing to inform you that a decision has been made with regards to your claim."

Holding breathe.................

"I am pleased to inform you that your claim has been successful and you will be receiving your money, plus interest. It will be in your account within 3 working days."

"Oh ....right.................thank you........"

And that was it, as simple as that, after all my worrying and struggles, that was it I had it!! It was a NICE pay-out. It was Ella's day to take me and you can guess what the main topic of conversation was, can't you? I had made a list while I was in hospital of what I was going to do with the money if I got it, people asked are you paying off a chunk of your mortgage? Hell no!!! This was going to be my trip money, my treat money, after everything that I had been through and was continuing to go through. I thought I am going to make the most of my time, however long that might be and I was going to go to as many places, see as many things as I could and experience as much as I could for as long as I could or for as long as the money lasted at any rate. It was a good day, all round because I managed to get another OU assignment sent off too.

Tuesday was a busy day, Deb one of the book club girls, took me for my treatment and we put the world to rights about bringing up children and life in general. My friend Tracey W, arrived shortly after I returned, all excited and nervous in equal measure because she was days away from getting married and she couldn't contain herself. Lisa arrived next for a catch up and she was equally as excited because she was looking at wedding venues for her wedding and she had asked me to be her bridesmaid, I was equally excited, I was so pleased for her. Tor took me again, on the Wednesday, we laughed about how Tor sees the world, she sees the fun in most things and she has such excitement and enthusiasm for things, it's contagious. When I got home, Deb, from the SSC, came to visit and we caught up on the gossip and goings on at work, I was eager to know if someone was in the library and if they had taken my job as it were; but I was surprised at hearing that it was still closed.

Kim took me on the Thursday and was definitely doing better on the motorways bless her, she just needs to be more confident that's all. On the Friday, Tes was taking me, but before my treatment, we had (I had) decided that we would go to Port Sunlight, which is very near to the hospital and it felt like a missed opportunity if we didn't. Now Tessa isn't known to be a lover of museums and the like, it's like asking a staunch football supporter to switch allegiances. So, I had left out some details, I hadn't explained what it was, so on the way when she asked I mumbled museum,

"Museum? MUSEUM?!"

"Well just a little one."

Actually, she really quite enjoyed it because a big part of the exhibition was in the form of a film, so it was ok. Afterwards we had some lunch there in the cafe, before then driving around the village which years before had been purposely built for the workers of the factory. It's an amazing place, go and see it if you get the chance. Then we went onto the hospital and after my treatment we normally had to wait for ages to see the doctor, so I asked the nurse if I could go home, instead of seeing the doctor and after asking me three times if I was ok she allowed us to go. The added bonus was that I didn't have to be weighed!

Each time I had a shower I worried that I would lose even more hair and showering on the Saturday I found that I had lost more hair, just above my ears but it wasn't as noticeable as the one on my forehead thank goodness. I had experimented clipping my hair in different ways so that it covered my bald bit but it was affecting my confidence. People said to me at the time; 'it will grow back' 'you can't see it' plus when I said I hated that I had put on so much weight 'it doesn't matter' 'you can't tell', to me it was one of the worst things. I hated putting on weight and now having a bald patch just added to my woes, it sounds trivial but the little confidence I had left was just being squashed by it all.

Later on, the Saturday was another afternoon tea, with Tes this time, at a local hotel 'The chimney house', we'd gotten a deal for it and considering what we had paid it was lovely, chilled and in beautiful surroundings too. So, another big tick. On the Sunday, I went to the pictures with Ella and Joanna, which was nice and chilled; Ella had wanted to go for food too but I was ready for home. She wants to fill all of her time but I needed a rest so reluctantly we went back home. Ella had applied to be an au pair but when I went into hospital, she pulled the plug on it all despite having spent money and time on the lengthy selection process. I had encouraged her to still do it but she wouldn't, so we had begun discussing doing some travelling together as another option. Ella Had always wanted to travel, I had too so when I was talking about adventures in a motorhome she seemed to be on the same page. The only thing which I was concerned about was that she had far more energy and get up and go than I had even in my 'before' days, she literally had 4 cylinders and I had 1 and on the odd occasion maybe 1.5!

On the Monday, it was Ella's shift again, I felt bad because she worked four long days and then took me on her day off but she was insistent. Today though I had organised a surprise for her, Ella loves eating out and trying new places, so after my treatment we went to Chester on the way back, to an amazing restaurant called Hickory's. It serves huge portions and we had ribs, there was enough leftover to take home a goody bag for Jack too. We were also treated to some tasters of shakes, as there was a barman training how to make them and we got some to try! All in all, we had had a very good day.

Deb took me again on the Tuesday, I was tired, so I just did nothing else at all when I got home. Wednesday was Tor and we talked at length about raising teenagers and how hard it is to get the balance right; you want them to learn and spread their wings but you don't want them to crash and burn, it's a delicate balance. It was also book club at night and we talked about going away for the weekend, after much discussion we decided upon Liverpool and I managed to find a lovely apartment right on the docks. As a thank you, for all their help and support I was going to treat them, with some of the money that I had received; I had decided that I would treat different people, as my way of saying thank you, for all the help and support, it was the least that I could do.

That night, in the middle of the night our house alarm went off, it's loud, very loud so despite wearing earplugs I got up and heard Jack shouting,

"Is there anybody there?"

From the top of the stairs, Terri was there and we just looked at each other,

"Stay there!"

He said putting his hand up to me, I couldn't help it I laughed.

"What are you doing?"

"Just checking no one is there....."

"Well if there was, they're hardly likely to shout yes!"

"It's to scare them!"

"I think that it's more likely that the alarm has been set off by a power cut than someone breaking in."

He went down to switch off the alarm but he then had to have a check about just in case we were being burgled, it was so funny despite being in the middle of the night. Ella hadn't made an appearance but she'd apparently heard it all from her bed.

The next day Elaine took me, we talked about the possibility of me going travelling and where to and what to see, I was so very excited by the prospect of travelling but until it was definite I didn't want to get too eager. On the Friday before my treatment, I had booked in to have reflexology with a former colleague who was retraining, she has now started her own business 'Trina Bailey therapies'. It's such a relaxing thing to have done, plus she could tell what was going on in my body, just from my feet, it's fascinating. Tes did the run to the Clatterbridge and after my treatment, I saw a different doctor not Dr Husband, there was only two more treatments and then I was done; he said that I would have a follow up appointment in a few weeks' time.

Once I got home, I had a look at some motorhomes, I was beginning to look at them so that I knew what I liked and what I didn't like but I wasn't ready to buy just yet, I'd allocated so much money to buy one but that actually gave me a very limited choice. Some were a ridiculous price, some new ones come in at a few thousand pounds and the ones in America are just out of this world. The other thing which I got organised was a trip to a Spa for me and Tessa, she had been the world's best chauffeur and had been really supportive and she truly deserved the treat. We had been to Hoar Cross Hall before and it is truly amazing, the food is 5 star, the bedrooms outstanding and the house and facilities were extravagant, so it would be great for both of us.

Mum and dad had arrived late on the Friday night, we had planned to go and watch a local production of 'Grease' altogether; we had lunch out, then we went to the theatre. There was mum, dad, Tes, Macy, Elaine and her daughter Maddie, Deb and her daughter Abbie, me, Els and Joanna, we were quite a party!! The show was amazing, Curtain Call are an amateur production company, however, they put on fantastic, professional standard productions, to rival most West End shows. On the Sunday, I only got up at 11 and I felt rotten, so I just had a very chilled day in my pyjamas. On top of everything else which was happening, I had lost my sense of smell, it had been awful since the operation. I did keep smelling this weird smell though, it wasn't really horrible, just odd and I couldn't figure out what it was; it seemed to follow me, so was it coming from me? Yet something else which needed sorting out?

On the Monday, after my treatment, I spoke to the nurse about how sick I was feeling and she recommended that I took my anti-sickness medication regularly and hopefully that should help. It was Ella's shift again, so after we went for lunch and then we went into a travel-agents to look at our options for a cruise. Whilst I was still in hospital I had decided that a cruise would be my first priority, Jack and Ella had been amazing, so supportive and they deserved a big treat, huge! I had also decided that if we were going to do it, then we were going all out, we were having a balcony and doing a Caribbean cruise. We sat down with an agent, who went through our options and basically it boiled down to two choices; one was an American company (so Ella wouldn't be able to drink because she would only be 19) and the other option was P and O, which as a British company she could legally drink from 18; also each cruise went to different places in the Caribbean. We didn't decide there and then, because I wasn't feeling great, but once we'd gotten home we quickly decided upon P and O!!

Tuesday the 31st of March was my last day of radiotherapy my dad took me; I'd got the nurses and staff some cupcakes as a thank you. And it was straight forward enough, after my treatment the nurses asked,

"Would you like to take your mask home?"

"My mask? What would I do with it, hang it on the wall?"

"Ha ha, I don't know but some people like to take them home."

It took me about 2 seconds to decide,

"No, I'm good thank you."

I was happy that my treatment had finished but from what the doctors had said that I wouldn't know for some time if it had actually worked, only time would tell.

Chapter 9

Treats and tests

When I got home from my last session, I booked the cruise, it was a kind of symbolic statement, to celebrate coming to the end of my treatment; but almost immediately I was questioning whether I had made the right choice of cabin. Ella and I are often sea-sick on boats but everyone had told me that the ships were so big that you barely knew that you were at sea. Ella wanted to know all the details of the cruise; where we were going, how we would get there, what our cabin was like, Jack on the other hand was happy to just go along with whatever was decided, we were talking about our cabin and Jack asked,

"What is my room like?"

"Eehhhhh?"

"My room?"

Ella and I just looked at each other, I answered,

"Jack we're all in the same room."

"What???"

"Yes there's 2 singles and a bunk."

"Oh nooooo.........what are the chances of me seeing a boob on this trip?!!"

He's hilarious even when he doesn't mean to be, he'd thought that he was going to have a room of his own bless him. I was spending enough as it was, I couldn't stretch to him having a room of his own, we would just have to be careful about keeping ourselves covered up. The good news didn't end there, I was on a roll, I had managed to get James Bay tickets for my birthday night, for us all to go; we all loved him and it was at Manchester Opera House, which is a great venue and not that big that the performers became dots in the distance either.

Tes came the following week, to cut my hair, during the treatment I hadn't been able to colour it and I had to wash it with baby shampoo so that it was gentle on my hair to help prevent any more from falling out. I had to make do with a cut which did help a little because it gone thin and lank, I wasn't sure if it was due to the treatment or the effects of the hormone damage. It was just something else that I had little control over, other than to follow the guidance of the nurses.

When mum and dad return back from Spain we always get together as a family and go out for a meal, the first chance we got this time was Friday 3rd; we went to a place in Sandbach called Café symphony, it had been recommended to us and it didn't disappoint. We had gorgeous food, we had a lovely helpful waitress, no niggles just lots of laughs, tasty, tempting sweets and I even had a couple of glasses of wine. I paid because it was our first real get together since my operation and radiation treatment, it felt nice to be able to treat people and everyone enjoyed their meals, so it was a roaring success.

The following day, I had arranged to go for a night away with one of my best friends Claire, she lived in Stockport and as a result we didn't meet up as much as we wanted. I got the train and remained vigilant because the last time I had gone on the train to meet her, I had somehow missed the stop for Stockport and I ended up in Manchester and had to get the next train back to Stockport. I hadn't been able to decide what to wear, so I'd packed for the apocalypse, including some wine! We were spending the night at Bredbury Hall because it was near to Claire and I was treating her because she had been a real support over the years for me and I had really relied on her at times. Our room was huge; it even had two double beds, we ordered some sandwiches and chilled in our room and while we got ready to go out for our meal, we drank some of the wine I had bought, from the plastic cups in the bathroom. We had a gorgeous meal in the restaurant and we even had a free bottle of wine, it was the most I'd drank in months and months. I'd taken several outfits and the one which I chose, I felt mildly confident in, I thought that if I was going to stay heavier I needed to get my head around it, accept the way I looked and just make the most of it. We had a laugh people watching, fuelled by the wine we even ventured into the club attached to the hotel; but we didn't last long, we just felt very out of place. I knew that I wasn't ready to meet anyone, I wasn't sure that I ever would be, I was a lot to take on.

I was back home, the following day by lunch and the kids were due out, we have a local Jazz festival and they were going there. I'd been in the past but I wasn't up to the crowds, the noise and the whole thing. Over the next few days I felt exhausted, so I just caught up on some TV and did a bit of reading. I was still feeling really sickie, the doctors had said that it could go on for a while; they had advised taking an anti-sickness medication regularly but I was already taking so many tablets, I was torn, I compromised by taking ½ a tablet instead of a full one. The trouble with a lot of medication is that there are side effects to taking them which all add to the symptoms and issues you are facing.

Tessa had booked a week away at a Caravan Park, by way of the Sun holiday deals, she's very on the ball with getting good deals and money off, it's a skill! Anyway, I wasn't originally going but she had asked me several times and to be honest I was ready for a change of scenery, at home I felt that I should keep going and still do the 'mum' duties and it was wearin me out. Don't get me wrong Jack and Ella were great, it was more the shift in my mind that had to be changed and adjusted to the 'new me' and what I could manage. Plus, it would give the kids a week off from worrying about me and seeing me trying and often failing to fight the fight, also mum and dad were going, so it would be nice to spend some quality time with them, so it seemed a good idea all round.

Mum and dad had gone to visit my auntie Jeanie and uncle Peter, who wasn't well, they live in Barmouth and so it was sort of in the same area as the caravan holiday. So, it was me, Macy and Tes was driving, and on the way we called at Llandudno for a break in our journey; we had lunch on the front and Tes and Macy had a wander up the pier, while I just enjoyed people watching. We arrived at the Hafan Y Mor caravan park mid-afternoon and we booked in, mum and dad arrived soon after, mum commented,

"It's not as good as the last one".

You see Tes has this skill and almost always gets us upgraded, but this time we were just in a normal van. It was great though, mum and dad had the main room, Tes and Macy had one bedroom and I had the other.

The following day, we had a trip to nearby Pwllheli, it was Grand National day and along with most of the country, it's a day when we place a bet; there is no great science to it, it's normally just the name of the horse which does it for me. We had a bit of a wander about I was using my crutch which just helped steady me and I took every opportunity to sit down too, but I was out and mobile, it was definitely progress. When we got back we had some lunch and settled down to watching the race, checking out the colours and number of the horses we had chosen so that we can keep an eye open for them during the race. During the race there is lots of screaming and shouting for our own horses and the inevitable grunts when they fell or were at the back; this time I was lucky mine came in 4th, so I barely got my money back, but it's fun to have one to cheer on, isn't it?

The day after, the weather was awful but we had archery to watch because dad and Macy were taking part; they were both pretty skilled, Macy particularly so. When they had finished we went on to the Mash and Barrel restaurant, those of us who could run ran over but me, mum and dad drove over in the car because the rain was coming down heavy. Afterwards, I spent some time doing some studying, I had taken it along because I needed to keep on top of it, now my brain was less foggy. In the evening, everyone went down to the club to play bingo, it frightens me, especially when I nearly have a line or house; one time I got a line but by the time I had checked it and shouted out, they had read out the next number so when they came over and checked, with the whole room watching they said I couldn't claim! So now I avoid playing. I was happy to stay behind for some quiet time because my family is great but they are sooooo loud.

One of our days there, we all went to see my aunt and uncle in Barmouth, my uncle has always been a larger than life character saying exactly what he thinks, my aunt is the sweetest person, she had always been so caring towards myself and my children whenever we had visited. We didn't get to see them that often but if we were in the area we always made a point of calling in on them, we had a fish chip lunch from a great chippy in town, which in the Summer has a huge queue outside.

The next few days were lovely, just lots of chilling, a bit of studying, tasty food, fun company; Tes is a great hostess too, so I did very little in the way of cooking or washing up. I hadn't done that much physically but my body was tired, my legs were weak and my body was jerking; I had begun to get used to feeling that way, if I did too much. I had to ration my energy so that I didn't miss out on everything, I was still learning how far I could push myself, it was all a delicate balance I hadn't quite mastered. It was part of getting used to my new status quo!

The following weekend Ella convinced me to go for some drinks with her, each objection was met with a counter argument,

"I'm not sure that I can really drink with all the medication."

"That's fine just see how you go, you could have one or two."

"I don't like it too busy."

"We're going in the afternoon, so it will be quiet."

"I don't have the energy to walk about."

"That's no problem, we will stay in one place."

I was out of arguments so I got changed and off we went. It was a beautiful, sunny day so we decided to choose somewhere with a nice outside area, we decided on 'the Cheshire Cat'; it is a really old pub, full of character and history. It was a place I went in my teens before I was 18 and allowed out properly; I have many, many happy memories of those times. It had little corridors forming shortcuts to different sections of the place and when I went with Elaine and my friend Diane, no one wanted to walk at the front because often the back two would sneak down one of the corridors without them realising. It had a small dance floor and a big dance floor and I spent a lot of time on both of them. I still went post 18 but there was often alcohol involved so my memories are cloudier!

We decided on some cocktails, I was thankful that I had had a good lunch at least. After a couple of hours and a couple more cocktails, soaking up the sun, we text Tes and she came to join the party. We had such a fab afternoon, it was chilled, relaxed, funny and entertaining. Kim was working in the town and finished work at 6pm, so we called on Kim to be a taxi for us, it must have taken some patience because we were all a little tipsy by this point. We had decided to go back to Tes and Kim's (they share a house) and continue our little impromptu party. Kim did a couple of shots to catch up and we'd called Jack round too. We ended up having a BBQ and enjoying the rest of the sun in the garden, in the end I was actually glad that Ella had made me go out.

A couple of days later, on Ella's day off, I'd agreed to go to a waterfall with her as she was off and wanted to do something. Someone had told her about it and had said that it was a beautiful area and the scenery was amazing; it was forecasted a gorgeous day, so we packed a picnic lunch and loaded up the car. It took nearly an hour and a half to get there and the last bit was a really windy road and we did question whether we were on the right track, but we turned a bend and saw some signs and it was glorious. We parked on the carpark, we were in a small valley with a river running through and there was a MOUNTAIN to climb.....it was actually a hill but to me it seemed like a mountain!

It was tough going and I struggled with the inclines and especially all the steps, I had my crutch but I was really struggling. After several breaks and with Ella pushing and pulling me, I sat down and said,

"Ella, I can't do any more I can barely breathe, you go on and leave me here."

"You've done really well."

"I know but I can't go any further, I think I might need mountain rescue."

Ella went to see how much further we had to go, while I sat and waited, planning my trip down.

"Mum it's literally just over there, come on you've come this far you can make it."

So, she pulled me up and all the way to the top, I truly didn't think I would or could do it but Ella doesn't see me like most people. Ella sees past the SICK person, to the person she wants or thinks or hopes I'll be; I'm not sure which but most of the time it does push me to do more and expect more from myself which is good but sometimes I want to say I feel shit, leave me alone girl! To be fair she knows me well and knows that I want to do things and push myself, she just gives me the opportunities.

At the top, there was a flat grassy area, the top of a waterfall ran into big pools of water and then after about 20m, it went over the top and straight down, I'm not sure how far because I didn't look, it was stunning and the noise from the waterfall was fantastic. We'd taken a great picnic with us, which we ate at the top, Ella then went off exploring and my job was to take some pictures of her, she really loves a waterfall and any kind of adventure; so she was climbing and balancing on top of things while I was stressing that she might fall in and go over the top of the waterfall. We spent a good hour or more at the top, it was so peaceful we pretty much had the place to ourselves, the only noise was the sound of the water. We had such a lovely time and weather being so glorious was a bonus.

When we came to come back down, we saw another way, which was a far easier way but we hadn't seen it before. We were half way back down, when we heard the thundering noise of a fast aeroplane flying over, it was a deafening noise, but because we were coming down into the valley we couldn't see it or the two others which flew over, if we had been at the top we would have seen it but I wasn't rushing back up. We finished off our day by having an ice-cream at the bottom of the waterfall. Needless to say, that I needed a lot of pain medication that night, the following day I could barely move; I don't remember the pain now but I do remember the fantastic waterfall.

The 1st of May brought another trip this time it was just me and Tes, I'd booked us a pamper break at Hoar Cross hall and Tes had managed to get us a free upgrade, I told you she has skills. We called at Trentham Gardens on the way, which is a lovely little shopping village and then we made our way to Hoar Cross. The first time, we had gone to Hoar Cross I was 7 months pregnant with Ella and it was a much smaller place, the next time, I had treated Tessa for a pre-wedding pamper; so, we knew the place and we knew that we wouldn't be disappointed. We had been upgraded to a suite and it was fabulous, we ate some lunch and went for a wander. We managed to find the slumber room, hidden away, which had these water type beds with covers and relaxing music, so we lay there trying not to fall asleep.

We hadn't booked any treatments because it would have been too complicated with everything that I had to explain but we had planned to try some of the classes they ran. My choice had been the relaxing Yoga, Tes reluctantly came along; it consisted of laying down and just relaxing, I knew Tes would hate it and she did,

"What was that?"

"Didn't you find it relaxing?"

"No, I nearly got up and left, don't make me do that again."

The food at Hoar Cross is to die for, breakfast and lunch are self-service but it is a 5-star buffet and evening meal is a three-course meal in the ballroom which is just magnificent. The following day we had planned on doing the meditation class, I'd only managed to convince Tessa to do it because in the brochure it said that it was done on the waterbeds in the slumber room, however, when the instructor arrived he explained that it wasn't in that room. After much discussion, Tes decided against it and went to a hula hoop class instead, I wish that I hadn't done it either, it was literally just breathing in and out, I could do that on my own! I was trying different things which I thought might help my recovery, so the next class that we tried was Tai Chi, which I'd always wanted to do. I found it tough, as my balance was off and my feet hurt, but I enjoyed the process, Tes as you can imagine hated it because it was way too slow for her.

We had a lovely chilled few days there, we had such a laugh and ate some gorgeous food too. On the last morning, before we left, we had one last visit to the spa area and then we got dried and dressed ready for home. Before we left we had a little walk in the gardens which go on for ever and there are little walks going off in different directions. We went off a little into a small wooded area and there was a hammock and Tes was eager to get in it, it's not an easy process but somehow I managed to get a video and then I also gave Tes a bit of a push and she wasn't so keen, the video is great though!

That evening when we returned I drove for the first time since November, Ella needed a lift out and I was the only person available, so I drove her car because mine didn't have tax or anything. It was like riding a bike, I didn't feel nervous at all. In truth no one had said that I couldn't drive, I had just chosen not to because I had been so weak and dizzy that I didn't think that I was safe to drive, but I was improving so maybe driving was the next step. I decided then as part of my progression, that I needed to get my car back on the road, it would give me some freedom and if I was thinking about going back to work I would need a car to get me there.

The next few days I did very little, I thought some days doing things and then some resting seemed to be a good plan. I did have a look at my last assignment, which carried a higher weight of marks than all of my other assignments and counted as a type of end of course exam. I was on track for a 2.1 but it would depend on what I got in this last assignment, so I was nervous and I paid particular attention to every detail. I even asked my friend Joanna to read it and give me some feedback because I wanted it to be my best piece of work. It was obviously somewhat harder because I wasn't fighting fit, I struggled to concentrate for any length of time, so I had to work for short bursts then give it a rest, then try again.

The following week, I had an appointment with my doctor, just a catch up and to speak to him about occupational health as he would have to sign off, that I was fit for work. He told me that he wouldn't sign anything until he knew the terms of my return to work, which was fair enough in the circumstances. I had lots of questions but he struggled to answer any of them, I was a complicated case and I probably knew more about my condition than he did, he couldn't possible know everything about every condition. It was at times like this that I really could have done with a specialist nurse who could answer my questions for me, but the one that the Clatterbridge had promised never materialised. To be fair some of my questions would have been difficult for anyone to answer because there were just too many variables; like when would I start to feel stronger? Could have any number of answers, the truth was, that it was a game of wait and see.

On the 8th I was back at the Clatterbridge for a check-up, dad took me and we had to wait for two hours to see the doctor; as we waited we got talking to the couple next to us and she thought dad was my husband, I know he looks young for his age but was I looking that rough? When we did get to see him, he had little to say. Due to my tumour being benign, the CT would show little difference in size, so there was really little to discuss because at that point no one knew if the radiotherapy had worked for me or not. I did ask him,

"If the tumour grows again, will I be able to have more radiotherapy?"

"No, we would have to explore other avenues."

Apparently, there is a maximum dosage that you can have in a lifetime and I had reached mine already. Another thing which I asked, was about the issue of my extreme tiredness and fatigue, he assured me that it was normal after radiotherapy and that it was likely to continue to last several more weeks. In truth, I was tired before, so it was tired, upon tired so it was to be expected.

The following day was Saturday, I had an appointment for another prolonged synacthen test, at the Royal in Liverpool,

'The long Synacthen test protocol was designed to confirm the diagnosis of primary adrenal failure. The diagnosis of adrenal failure is made on the cortisol response to ACTH at 30 min (see short Synacthen test). The prolonged stimulation of the adrenals by ACTH in this test results in a degree of recovery by adrenal glands which have become atrophic due to pituitary failure; whereas, adrenal glands that are themselves diseased will not respond.'

I'd had the test several times before, so I knew that it wasn't a pleasant test at all. Tests weren't usually carried out on a Saturday but the lovely nurses and the doctor had come in especially, to do these tests. There were two other ladies, a man and myself, dad dropped me off and went to visit a

118

cousin who lived in Liverpool. As was normal for me things didn't go quite to plan, the nurses couldn't get a vein; they couldn't on the 2nd attempt, the 3rd, on the 4th attempt the doctor was called and he succeeded but somehow there was loads of blood everywhere, over the sheet they put on you to protect the covers on the bed. They take blood firstly to check your levels before they give you the medication to stress out your system, after they give you the stressing medication it should force your body's blood sugar below 2. However, as was always the case with me, my blood sugar didn't go down enough; it only went down to 2.8 at which point they should have given me another dose to force it further down, but they didn't as the doctor was busy.

So, when they did give me the additional dose, my blood sugar had gone up to 3.7 and 2nd 3.9 but between the two I think my blood sugar had dropped further as I was very symptomatic; you feel really hot and sweaty, you feel really tired and just dizzy and weird, but I think that they missed it, normally when doing this test, you have one person with you at all times. So, after my 2nd dose it dropped to 2.9 and despite me feeling worse and very symptomatic it went to 3.1 then back down again to 2.8, then up again. I wasn't sure that the data would be correct because the test had been all over the place, so the test finished without a suitable conclusion to one part at least. I always feel rough afterwards, I felt very shaky and tired and I slept on the way home, and for another hour and a half when I got home.

Over the weeks I had had so many visitors, all of my friends came regularly and even people I didn't see that often, as ever I felt so privileged to have so many people who cared.

I had a very chilled week because I really was just exhausted I was still trying to do more than I should and I wasn't getting the balance quite right. I basically watched lots of TV and did very little at all, I even put off having a shower because it tired me out so much, but I could only do that so long otherwise I would smell!

On the Friday the 15th, I had a fields of vision test at local eye clinic at the hospital,

'A visual field test is an eye examination that can detect dysfunction in central and peripheral vision which may be caused by various medical conditions such as glaucoma, stroke, pituitary disease, brain tumours or other neurological deficits.'

My tumour sits right on my optic nerve, so there is real a concern that it will affect my vision, so being monitored by the clinic is reassuring. I have worn glasses since I was 14 and over time, I wore them more and more, until I was wearing them all of the time. I had some awful glasses in the 90s, I had permed hair and big glasses and looking back I looked like Deirdre Barlow from Coronation Street; I switched to contacts about 15 years ago. I was very fortunate that I had a great optician in Specsavers too, I found that they too monitored my vision and eye health extremely well. For the fields of vision test you have one eye covered and you look at a light, in a little chamber and you buzz each time that you see a light flash, somewhere else in the chamber, it is a painless process and quickly over and done.

The following day Ella took me to Sheila's house, she was the lady who I had met in hospital and Suzie who I had also met would be there too. Sheila was having a get together for her birthday, there were many people there who I didn't know, but everyone mixed and chatted away happily. What struck me was the amount of people who had experienced a significant illness, so it was interesting to hear people's stories of triumph and battle; so many strong women who had overcome and were living their lives to the full. Again, I was struck by how illness affects people, most people come out the other side with more fight to live each day to the max, it would be good if we could do that without the illness prompting us to do it!

The following day I watched 'The C word' starring Sheridan Smith, it is the true story of a woman's battle with breast cancer. At one point, she said that 'she just wanted to be over this bit, so that she could just get on with living her life.' My first thought was, that's exactly how I felt, my recovery just seemed to be taking so long to me, everyone else said it was no time at all. I think that a big part of me was struggling with the idea that I would never be back to my 'normal', I may get somewhat better but maybe not enough and that was still a bitter-sweet pill to swallow for me. Then as I continued to watch; after getting cancer for the second time, she died and I had to think, well I AM still here, living to fight another day.

Then as I was feeling moved by the film, contemplating it's message, Ella came in, she had found a new feature on her phone which played back action in slow motion, we spent a good while filming different actions such as Ella shaking her bum or me my arm and then playing them back in slow motion. We laughed so hard that I couldn't catch my breath. I do love moments like that, they are priceless moments of joy.

Chapter 10

D day

I had the results of my blood tests, I have had copies of all my tests for as long as I can remember, I like to record what is 'normal' for me and what is of concern; these latest tests showed that something wasn't quite right. It looked like I could be anaemic and there was an issue with my kidneys too, on my bloods taken the 1st of April it showed that I had a eGFR score of 59, it was low but I thought that it had been a one off but this blood result was again low at 61. Before my operation my eGFR was above 90 and since the operation it had been coming down gradually as my creatine went up from in the 60s to in the 90s.

'eGFR or Calculated Creatinine Clearance is a simple test to detect early changes in kidney function. A normal result means that kidney disease is less likely while a low value suggests that some kidney damage has occurred. Significant decline of the GFR from a previous test result can be an early indicator of kidney disease requiring medical intervention.

0) Normal kidney function – GFR above 90 mL/min/1.73 m^2 and no proteinuria

1) CKD1 – GFR above 90 mL/min/1.73 m² with evidence of kidney damage

2) CKD2 (mild) – GFR of 60 to 89 mL/min/1.73 m² with evidence of kidney damage

3) CKD3 (moderate) – GFR of 30 to 59 mL/min/1.73 m²

4) CKD4 (severe) – GFR of 15 to 29 mL/min/1.73 m²

5) CKD5 kidney failure - GFR less than 15 mL/min/1.73 m²'

Luckily, I had my appointment with my surgeon and the endocrine consultant the following week, so I thought that at least I can ask some questions and hopefully get some answers. The main thing was getting the pain managed and the source of my excessive weight gain identified and addressed.

20th May 2015, Well it's D day!!! It was more than 6 months since I had had my operation and I was back at the Walton Centre. I'd organised my medical notes to take with me, mum and dad were my escort's for the day. I had my MRI first – but as was the norm, the nurses struggled to get a vein for the injection, it took 3 attempts before they were successful. After my MRI, we all had a quick sandwich for lunch and waited patiently to see Mr. Sinha; when we walked into the room a new consultant introduced himself Dr. Zaidi, he apologised explaining that Mr. Sinha was running late. So, we began going through all my hormone test results; there was again an issue with my cortisol, my growth hormone, maybe my thyroid and definitely my pee!! He said that I would need yet more hormone tests and retests for some that I'd had done at the doctors which weren't what they had expected.

When Mr. Sinha arrived, he was very apologetic, he couldn't bring up the MRI pictures like he normally did but he explained that the tumour was still present, but it was now about the size of a small pea rather than the size of walnut!! He said he was happy to check up on me in 6 months time,

"I'm going on a cruise in January will it be before then?"

"No, I think we'll make it for when you get back."

I'd have liked another check-up before Christmas and my long-haul flight for the cruise but I wasn't going to argue, he knew best. Before I left, I had to have more blood tests and it took ages to get and it bloody hurt. All in all, I was fairly happy with everything, I was glad that they were going to be checking and keeping an eye on my levels and hormone function and that the tumour hadn't grown; I hadn't expected miracles, I had learned to expect little from my visits and then anything more was a bonus. When I got home Tes turned up with flowers, I wrote this in my diary,

'Tes turned up with some lovely flowers for me, Ella and I had only said when we saw Sheila's flowers, how lovely it had been to have such lovely flowers. I'd had a more or less constant stream of flowers given to me since I had gotten out of hospital and that was months before now. It was strange, I rarely had two lots at any one time, just as one set of flowers was nearing the end of its bloom, I would somehow get another bunch from someone.'

About that time, I was desperately trying to finish my final assignment and get it posted off, all the other assignments I had been able to send off electronically but for some reason the final one had to be printed and posted. I could only print on my printer one sided but Tes could print both sides, so I sent it over to her for her to print. When I called to pick it up, it was all wrong the text was too big and it was formatted wrong, so I had to go back home and just print it one sided. It cost me £7 to post it, if it wasn't there by the correct day, that was it, your assignment would be void, so it was quite a significant task. However, once it was posted and on its way, I was done, I had spent the best part of 4 years studying and I now I just had to wait for my grading, it was a huge relief that it was finished because I didn't have the pressure to study when I wasn't feeling great.

On the 23rd May I caught up with my SSC (secret saddo club) Gemma, Deb and Claire. We tend to meet up during holidays because everyone is so busy, we have to plan weeks in advance, we normally go to Manchester and have a few drinks, something nice to eat and catch a train home again, early evening. It was another great day, full of laughter, gossip and normally conversations about sex and poo, for reasons I don't know!!

During the half term break, I was also going away with Joanna to Chester for a couple of days, we planned lots of chilling, great food, some cocktails and lots of sleep. On the first day, we just booked in and had a little wander about Chester before having a nice meal out, with a couple of wines. On the second day, we'd spent time in the hotel's spa and then we went out for lunch, along with some cocktails, they were 2 for 1 so it would be criminal not to! By the time we were done, we were a bit tipsy and it was 5 o'clock, so we decided rather than go back, get changed and go back out for tea; we'd just get nibbles and just chill in our room. We decided to treat ourselves and go to M & S because they have some lovely food; we got some good quality nibbles. Now to say that we were a little giggly, because of the drinks we'd had for lunch, is a bit of an understatement, so rather than walk round M & S sensibly we ended up running around all excited.

"Ohhhh Joanna look at this it has chocolate and fruit in!"

Then we'd run off again and at one point we lost each other,

"ANNA..........Anna ...."

Joanna was calling me in that loud whisper type of voice, we were just being daft and laughing at ourselves and it was fun, plus I think that I was more than happy that I didn't have to go out again. So, we returned to the hotel and watched a film and ate our nibbles in our pyjamas. The following day, on our way home we called at Cheshire Oaks, a designer retail outlet, I needed some nice outfits because I couldn't get in a lot of mine because I had put on so much weight. We chose a handful of shops, so that we didn't do much walking and we had a look around; I managed to find a jumpsuit that I liked and then I decided to try on a dress which I liked. I got it on just, but when I came to get it off, it somehow it got stuck, luckily Joanna had been waiting by the changing room so I called her. She tried without success, so I was stood there with my arms up and dress stuck around my shoulders unable to go back or forth. Joanna managed to get the attention of one of the assistants who had a try and then she called for more help, oh great more people to see my pants! By this point Joanna had lost it completely and was doubled up laughing, luckily, somehow, the assistants got me out of my dress. Funnily enough I didn't buy it or try anything else on!

At the end of the May, Ella was off to her favourite City of Dublin for the weekend, my dad had gone with Tes and Macy to a ranch in Arizona for a couple of weeks. Macy is a great horse woman and so they had decided to go to this ranch, where she could ride several times a day, dad and Tes just did the odd ride and spent most of their time by the pool I think. While the cat was away (dad) me and mum had decided to go on our own mini adventure. I still hadn't sorted my car and insurance, so mum had to drive, she drives but she doesn't really like driving too far but we didn't have a choice. Our first point of call was Barmouth, we stopped off at the fabulous 'Rhug shop' for a look around and a wee and then we stopped off at Bala for some lunch. I have travelled this journey many times and every time I am reminded what a beautiful country we have, it's even better when it's a beautiful day!

My uncle Peter looked brighter than the last time we had seen him and it was nice to catch up with him and my auntie Jeannie, we stayed a few hours with them, before moving on. We had decided that we would move on from there and not stop over because we had a schedule, so we travelled to the 'Wild pheasant' on the outskirts of Llangollen. It was a nice enough place and we had our tea in the pub and a couple of drinks before going back to our room. The following morning, we had planned to go to the Roman settlement, at Wroxeter, which had been my choice because I had watched a TV programme on the building of the Roman villa on the site. I had high expectations but to be honest it was a bit of a let-down, it wasn't as impressive as I thought it would be and it was a dark, miserable day so that didn't help either. We'd planned to spend longer there but instead, we set off for our next destination which was The National Memorial Arboretum, which is a collection of memorials based around war and conflict, near Litchfield. We had planned to go the following day but we had time to kill, because we couldn't book into our guest house until later.

First impressions were fantastic, as we parked up there was a mini bus full of soldiers getting out, we later learned that soldiers maintained the memorials, they had come to clean up the memorial which belonged to their company. We got a little train which takes you around the site, showing all the different memorials and monuments, it is quite a big site so we were grateful for the train ride; I took lots of pictures namely of the Irish guards one, which my paternal grandad was a soldier with. There is a central monument which lists the names of soldiers killed since the second world war, it is a magnificent memorial and very moving, we were fortunate to get a lift up to it by a man in a little buggy, I think that he saw my crutch and took pity on us. There is also a little chapel on site, so we had a look in there too, it was very beautiful and peaceful. We finished up with a cup of tea in the café and the place was probably half full with service men and ex- service men, we took our time because we were still too early to book in.

We managed to find the little guest house we had booked, with little issue, but there was no one home, so we sat in the car looking at the book we had bought about the Arboretum, until the lady arrived home. When she did, there was us, plus some other guests who had been waiting too and we were treated to tea and cake, so it was worth the wait. Within the little group, there were a couple of ex-soldiers, we said that we had already been but that we were returning for the ceremony the following day, they shared their stories with us, it was fascinating speaking with them. It was a B & B and was just a big house with rooms rented out, we had booked one with an ensuite but we had to share a double bed! The following morning, we had an amazing breakfast of poached eggs on toast with fruit to start, everyone sat around a big dining table; there was an elderly gentleman, who he was carrying a flag at the service, so we said that we would keep an eye open for him.

We were at the memorial for before 10am, as there was a special service going on so we knew that it was going to be busy. When we arrived, there was already a lot of people milling around, so we thought that we would head for the memorial and see if we could find a seat, there were seats laid out but they were obviously for people who had been invited as it were, but we managed to find a bench with a good view. There was a procession with a band playing, it was for a rededication ceremony and there were lots of soldiers there; the serving soldiers were all in uniform and the veterans all had their medals pinned onto their jackets. We had such a lovely morning watching the service, it was very impressive and moving.

We called for lunch once we were back in Crewe, I'd had such a lovely time with my mum and our mini break, I was thankful we had made it home in one peace; mum drove like driving Miss Daisy on the straight and on the bends like Nigel Mansell, plus she thought that she owned the roundabouts! Bless her though, she did it, she hadn't wanted to but it was needs must because we couldn't get trains to where we needed to go. After lunch, I was due to have an appointment with an occupational health doctor, at a nearby office complex. The doctor called me in and she was very nice; she asked lots and lots of questions and I was worried that she would say that I couldn't return to work, but in the end, she agreed that I could, but on a very reduced timetable. By this point it was June, I knew that I wasn't fit enough to work full time or anywhere near that but I thought it would be good to make a start and get a feel for my new job. My thinking was, that if I made a start I could recoup over the six-week Summer break and then come back stronger. I spent the next few days just doing nothing my body needed the rest.

My next outing was to pick up my 'fit for work' note from the doctors which he had done after I had assured him that it would be on a very gradual basis, so he made that a specification on the form. My next port of call was to see the head at my school, in my absence the headteacher had left and the deputy had been appointed as the new head, so thankfully he knew me and I knew him. Jason, the new head, was eager to assure me that they, as a school, would accommodate me as much as they could, he even said that they would write the job description around me, so I was more than happy with the meeting, I was ecstatic. I hadn't realised that the library had still not been opened, they were waiting for me to return, which I was really surprised by. I felt excited about starting a new type of role and seeing how it worked for me, now that I had finished my OU studies I was eager to find a focus elsewhere.

In the afternoon while I was reading I had these weird flashes in my left eye, something which I had not had before; days later I went to the opticians and they told me that I had 'posterior vitreous detachment', to be honest the optician looked about 12, so I wasn't totally convinced of his assessment, but if he was right then it's something else to add to the list. Then over the weekend, I had a really bad bout of dizziness, sometimes it creeps up on me and other times it just comes out of the blue and I still don't really know what causes it; was it something to do with my cortisol levels, could it be that I had been doing too much or could it just be one of those things? It was typical though because my first day back at work was just two days away! Tes had sent some clothes she was throwing away some I wouldn't wear and the rest wouldn't fit, this is what I wrote in my diary,

'I HATE, HATE, HATE being this fat and no I don't care that it's down to hormones medication etc. and I don't want to hear well at least you're here. I bloody hate being this fat. Once I've got things back on track I will love my body and appreciate it far more lol.'

It sounds vain and petty but it was and still is an issue for me, I had been fairly stable with my weight for most of my adult life. Over time I had added extra pounds but not like this weight I had gained, I had gained about 2.5 stone, so when people said they couldn't tell, I knew that they were just being kind, because often I looked about 6 months pregnant. It's like when people say you look good then weeks later they would say 'oh god you looked awful', but no one wants to say for fear of upsetting, which is good I suppose. What is difficult is when people say 'Oh you look great' and sometimes you just want to say ' I feel like crap'! Invisible illnesses are tough!

Chapter 11

Back to work

Ella and I had talked about sharing her car, but it would mean that I would have to get up really early to drop her at work and I just thought, that wouldn't be great because one thing I did need, was lots of sleep. So, I sorted my car insurance and tax so that I would have my car, ready to go back to work. Typically, the night before my first day back, Tuesday the 9th of June, I had the worst night's sleep, then I had to have a blood test before I went in; I have to have them every few months to keep a check on everything. I went into work and I went to see the people I knew and I had a catch up; Deb, who was the only other member of the SSC still at the school, Tracey who I had kept in touch with and then Helen and Steve who had taken over running the unit, that I had previously managed. I'd been told that another member of staff had started sorting out the library and I did manage a catch up with her, Ursula but I wasn't sure if she was just there for a bit or if she would be there with me. I'd only done a couple of hours but it was enough, there was a lot to catch up on.

Back home I had a nap, I'd not had one in a few weeks but I suppose it was understandable. Later when I was getting some tea sorted, I began to feel really sickie, then I had to sit down quickly because I thought that I was going to pass out, my heart was racing and I was feeling like I did when I first came out of hospital. Then I realised that I hadn't taken my

2pm steroid, idiot! The following day, I had to rest up and then the next day at work I had a meeting; I was anxious that we were not all on the same page with regards to what the 'Learning resource Centre' (Library). I had had discussions with Jason, the head, he wanted a more integrated unit, which pushed the literacy agenda into all departments, so that children were using their skills in all subjects; but I wasn't sure that he had discussed it with anyone else. We talked mainly about accelerated learning, a new initiative, which was essentially a reading programme. It was only when I brought up information literacy that we talked about it, I was just confused as to where I fit in, but it was only my second day, again I needed to be patient!

At the weekend, I was going away with the book club girls; Elaine, Deb, Tor and Joanna. Elaine, Deb and myself went in the morning and on the train, we sat with an old lady, who turned out to an ex nurse who'd worked at Clatterbridge Hospital, so we ended up talking about my illness a little. Small world. Then she was regaling us with stories of her life, she was 73 and she looked amazing; I hope that I have that much zest for life at her age. We got a taxi to the BLOCK where we were staying, we had a chatty taxi driver who gave us a guided tour on the way, apparently, it's called party towers; so much for booking a nice place. We left our bags and went into town for lunch, we called for some supplies of food and drink on the way back and we booked in; the apartment was nice apart from not enough seating and no door on the ensuite bathroom. We'd planned to dump the stuff and go back out but we never moved, we just sat nattering until Tor and Joanna arrived about 6.30. We had a quick catch up with the cocktails we'd bought and then we freshened up and went out about 8.45; we'd planned to go to the smuggler's cove but couldn't get a table. We ended up in a place called 'What's cookin', not far from the apartment block, which was great; the food was lovely, there was a great atmosphere and we had a great time. Just as we were going back to the apartment about 10.30, there was a group of lads just going out, oh to be young!

On the Saturday, we just sat around for most of the morning eating strawberries, toast and drinking tea, while nattering away; we finally got moving about 11.30. We walked to the Albert dock area and we had a look around the Liverpool museum, it's a fascinating place and free to boot. There was an awkward moment when we were waiting for a lift and the doors opened and two people were snogging away, I went to go in and noticed them and I said an embarrassed, 'Sorry' and the doors closed. We were all a bit emotional about the evacuee area of the museum, reading and watching footage and hearing how badly some of them were treated. Some of them, should never have been sent in the first place, because they had families, most were never reunited with their families.

It was another beautiful sunny day, so next we decided to get some ice-creams and sit on the front soaking up the sun and watching the world go by. The city was busy and we tried to find somewhere to sit outside but after lots of faffing, we ended up back at the docks at 'What's Cookin' again, we had another gorgeous meal, some of the girls went to buy some supplies, but I ended up back at the apt by 6!!! I know it's sort of pathetic but it suited me, I got straight into my pj's. No one seemed that bothered about going out, although we did say that next time maybe we should make a bit more of an effort. We had an evening of watching films, eating snacks and just having a laugh; by 10 I was well ready for bed, the others were a little disappointed I think but I knew I would be fit for nothing if I didn't go to bed.

The following day, we woke to the noise of loudspeakers and music, it turned out that there was a half marathon going on and passing outside of our window; so we watched lots of people running by, all sorts of people. Then we got dressed ready for the off, we went to the Maritime museum but my body was struggling a little, so I took every opportunity to sit down that I could. Again, it is another fabulous museum and again, it's free. For lunch, we went to 'Blue' on the Albert dock, we all had a roast dinner and it was truly the best roast dinner that I have ever tasted, with the most amazing gravy, which is always a bonus. Then I had my favourite dessert, cheese cake and that too was gorgeous. After, we made our way back to the station for our train; we'd had so many funny moments, it had been great, exhausting but great.

The next day, I was back in work, as you can imagine my body was objecting, I still felt a bit lost, I didn't know what I should be focused on. I acknowledged that there were lots of changes and updates going on but I suppose it just wasn't what I had expected, I'm not sure what I had expected: it was a new role that was being created, so it would take some time to figure out what it would be, but as ever I was trying to run before I could walk. My horoscope for the day -

'Whether the changes about to take place at work have been instigated by you or forced upon you by others, they'll make life easier in the long run. For now, though you may just have to grin n bear it. Don't let a minor dissent escalate into a major battle.'

How weird is that? Maybe I should just get on with it and have an easy life BUT that's not me, I wanted a challenge and to know what was expected of me. It was difficult for people at work because they didn't want to pressure me or push me too hard but as ever I was impatient, I should have just been thankful that they were being so nice to me.

In the afternoon, Tes dropped me off at the eye clinic, I thought it was going to be a waste of time but they put the drops in, which make your pupils go big. Then the doctor examined me and she put this stuff in, which numbed my left eyeball, she then placed a little microscope thing with a bright light, right onto my eye, freaky and not very comfy. Any way I did have POSTERIOR VITREOUS DETACHMENT, so the boy optician had been right!! It's apparently common with people with short sightedness, it's the jelly like stuff becoming detached causing flashes and floaters.

'A posterior vitreous detachment (PVD) is a condition of the eye in which the vitreous membrane separates from the retina. It refers to the separation of the posterior hyaloid membrane from the retina anywhere posterior to the vitreous base'

I had to watch what I'm carrying and if I see more flashes and floaters I have to get back in touch as an emergency. But this is very unlikely!! (with me it's more bloody likely lol) all I thought was, good god something else, I'm falling apart.

The following day I was off again; I had things which I felt that I needed to do, so I'd do a bit then sit quietly, I could quite easily have just lay down all day; the thought of work made me want to cry. Someone said to me, 'we as women just get on with things whatever life throws at us', and I was sat just thinking, I'm exhausted at having to do that day in day out, I'm fed up with it, I want some time out. I couldn't blame anyone but myself I had pushed everyone into agreeing with me going back to work and now I was already having doubts about it but I did have some leeway because of my phased return. I had another quick nap in the afternoon because I was that tired, they were definitely becoming more frequent; I had gotten out of the habit of having a sleep before I went back to work. On my way to work the next day I picked up my friend Tracey, Hutch, because she had broken her arm and couldn't drive. When I got in, I caught up on emails and applied for two courses which would help me in my new role, I sorted out my computer so I could access everything. Then I went through some books which needed clearing out, I felt like I had achieved something and I was feeling more organised. I left at 12 with Trace, I'd only done two hours but I was tired, but surely that was to be expected? I'd not worked for nearly 12 months, so getting back into the swing of things was going to take it out of me.

At work on the Friday, I was again feeling lost and without much direction, then on the way home Tracey said that there was going to be restructuring of staff, at work and there would be redundancies. It got me thinking, could I manage if I wasn't working? I totted up my outgoings and incomings; I wasn't going out, out, so other than my holidays I wasn't really spending lots. I just didn't want to let people down and to keep battling on, when in my heart I felt like I couldn't make it work; it was just proving to be harder than I'd anticipated. The work was straightforward and there weren't the stresses there had been when I had managed the behaviour unit but I was still exhausted by the work. I was needing to have naps again, for every hour that I worked, I was napping the same amount, I couldn't do that if my hours increased, how could I cope with full-time?

The next week I had planned to speak with the head just to clarify my position; when I eventually had my meeting, I began by saying my initial reason for wanting the meeting was to discuss the direction of the unit. I said it was a big job, which I wasn't sure I was up to. I explained that the thought of working full time come September felt like climbing Everest. I tried to explain that because of the restructuring I didn't want to keep my role and then come back in September and say I can't do this; meaning someone had then lost their job and they would yet again, be without a key role filled. I hoped that it came across as I wanted what was fair and not that I just wanted the redundancy because it really wasn't about that, it was more that I didn't want to mess people about. It wasn't what he was expecting, he asked if there was anything that he could do to help with the situation, but I assured him that I was more than happy with the support that I had been given; so he said he would look at options and come back to me.

The following day, I went to work as usual and when I got back Jack was home and he'd done a load of work around the house which was great, since being ill I hadn't been able to keep on top of things so coming hope to a lovely, freshly cleaned house was fantastic. The following day at work, I received an email from the finance lady to come for a talk about my proposal to finish, she wanted to check that I wasn't being pushed out and I explained that that wasn't the case, we discussed it and she came up with a solution. It was perfect for me, I could finish in July and then I'd be done. I did mention about group work and possibly coming back in and she said do it and charge consultancy rates, you'll get more money! I felt like a weight had been lifted because now I'd have some breathing space and some time to properly recuperate. I went home for a nap yet again, but happier in the knowledge that I wouldn't have the pressure of work hanging over me for much longer. I knew that I was very fortunate, that I was being able to finish and that in the short term I didn't have to worry about earning money.

Since deciding to buy a motorhome I had looked at so many on Ebay, to figure out what it was that I actually wanted; if Ella and I were going to be spending a chunk of time in it, I didn't want to be making up beds each night, so ideally, I was looking for two sleeping areas and an area to eat too. I had a list of criteria, which my friend Sarah (another old dancing friend), had given me to look for; diesel, at least 2.5L, turbo if possible, an oven and I also wanted one which had a fairly low mileage. It had proved to be a confusing and frustrating process, I just wanted someone to come along and say 'Hey Anna, what about this?' Plus, the insurance was proving to be quite difficult too because of Ella's age very few would cover her, but I had sort of expected that. I'd looked at lots and lots and I'd seen one which seemed to fit my criteria, it was a bit dated but I knew that I could spruce it up.

Saturday the 20th June, me, Tes, Jack and Macy went to have a look at the motorhome which I liked, it was near Rhyl so an hour or so from us. We all had a look round and I really liked it and the lady seemed genuine enough, it had everything that I wanted, except power steering which I could get done. I priced up the insurance and including dad and Ella it was going to cost about £1000 which was what I'd sort of thought it would be. It had really low mileage for its age and it also had 12 months MOT too. On the way back, we talked about it and when I got home I phoned Sally who owned the motorhome and I offered £8300 and she bit my hand off; it was only when I put the phone down that I realised the asking price was £7500, so I had offered way over the asking price, so I messaged her,

'Hi Sally I've come off the phone and my son has pointed out that I offered 8300 I meant 7300. I'm really sorry and don't want to mess you about, what figure would you be happy with I have a little leeway. I really would like the van. '

She replied, 'Hi there. I thought you'd made a mistake...... I'd really like the £7500 but I'd throw in the extra awning I bought for £250 last year, used once or £7400 without the awning?'

142

In the end, I agreed to pay £7500 and take the awning to; I priced up the powered steering and I'd get it fitted as soon as I picked up the motorhome. We picked it up the following weekend, Saturday 27th, but again I nearly made a boob with the payment, it kept refusing my online banking payment, then I nearly clicked 75,000 rather than 7,500!! The plan was for me and Tes to drive down and get the powered steering fitted straight off. I drove a little of the way and Tes drove from Stafford services. We only got a little lost in Stratford itself, we had just missed our turning to the place where the van was being done, so we went to the end of the street and had to use a pub car park to turn the van around, then some bloke told us off for going up a one-way street .... It was about 2 feet!! We arrived and as the mechanic wasn't around we promptly went off to the pub for food and cider in the sun. On coming back, we met Chris, the mechanic, he plugged us into his electrics because the plan was that we would stay over-night and he would do the work the following day. I said

"Do you want to have a look at it now?"

"If that's ok? I'll make a start on it."

He then spent an hour fiddling with it while me and Tes got the beds sorted and just as we put the DVD on he finished up; it was a good job really because we were watching '50 shades of grey', he would have wondered what all the noise was!

Chris was up and about by 8.30 working away outside, but we had to get up because he would need access to the inside too. It was peeing it down so we decided to have another brew and wait for it to ease a little, by 9.45 he had started making lots of noise so we decided to get going. Chris said that Anne Hathaway's cottage was just around the corner, with a cafe opposite, so we walked round and paid £9.50 each! (well I paid 19!) And it was a pitiful crappy house and gardens that weren't even there when she lived there; as I've said before Tes doesn't do museums, so as you'd expect she was less than impressed and she complained saying,

"It was false advertising, saying that it is Anne Hathaway's cottage, she only actually lived here for a few years."

The poor woman didn't know what to say, I was in the other room, cringing but to be fair it was an overpriced affair. We did have a laugh though. We then walked into town, by this time the rain had eased off, we found a little cafe and had a great bacon bap and brew, it was lovely because we were knackered and hungry. We had a mooch around the town and got a taxi back to the van, luckily Chris was just finishing up, so it was perfect timing. We made our way home and by the time I had dropped the van in storage it was 5pm and I could easily have gone straight to bed.

Chapter 12

Last days at work

I love the theatre and I had managed to get cheap tickets for a local show, Tes picked me up and drove to the Regent in Hanley. We didn't know the musical LOVE ME TENDER but it turned out to be all Elvis' songs, so we knew that we'd like the music, we'd grown up on it. It was brilliant, we absolutely loved it, great cast, music, story and so so funny. It's a shame mum and dad had missed out, we'd have taken them along if we'd known. I didn't normally go out on a 'school' night but it had been well worth it, I'd had a nap and taken extra hydrocortisone which I did whenever I had a long tough day.

After a few more days spent at work going through the motions, I was off for a weekend in Brighton for a hen do, it was a friend of Joanna's really but I'd agreed to go along, but my feet were killing me and they had become quite swollen too of late, so I was a bit wary of how much walking there might be. We were going to London and then onto Brighton, we had a lovely time on the train because we were spoilt in first class. We were staying in a 3-story house as there were 13 of us, we all grabbed a room in the house, Joanna and I got a lovely twin on the ground floor with a little ensuite. We quickly unpacked and then set off out exploring, we ended up on the nearby beach but in a bar rather than having a paddle!!

It was an absolute scorcher of a day, so as you can imagine it was heaving with people having a drink on a Friday afternoon.

There was no plan in place as to what we were doing, whether we were staying out or going back and going out later, in the end someone made a decision that we would go back and go out again later. So, I left the 'party' and went back to the house for a nap, in the end I had a rest rather than a sleep but I still felt better for it. It was nearly 9 before we made a move to go out, but there hadn't been a restaurant booked for us, so we couldn't get a table anywhere, we ended up in a taco shop which was more like a takeaway with seats, the food was good but that was it. Myself and another girl who wasn't feeling well, came home at about 10ish and had a brew and natter until 11. The others came in about 1am, I was fast asleep.

I was awake and up for a brew by 9.30, some girls were ready for the off but others were still in bed. It seemed that people were doing their own thing, so, Joanna and I went off and had a mooch down 'the lanes' and then onto the pier, where we took daft pictures and people watched and had a laugh. We met up with most of the others for lunch, fish n chips on the front which was lovely, it was proper seaside fare. Everyone went their own way again, we called to get cake and came back for a lovely nap I had about 2 hours. That night we were booked in for cocktail making which was ace, the lad doing it had his hands full but he was very witty and quick with his come backs, so it made for a very entertaining hour or so. After we were shown to our own private area in another part of the pub, I was just thankful that there were seats! As part of the cocktail making deal, food was included, it turned out to be a few slices of pizza and nibbles.

I'd lost any confidence I'd had with men; since being ill but especially since putting on weight and not going out so much, so it was just window shopping for me. Most of us moved on to another bar, I'd had a couple of drinks but some had had a lot more and it was funny watching their antics on the dance floor. I had a dance but I conserved my energy for songs that I really knew and loved; I was messing about on my third turn on the floor and somehow I managed to pull my calf muscle! I came home gone 1am which is the longest I think I'd stayed out in years, I hobbled back with two other girls who had had enough. Next morning, we walked in search of brunch, we found an all-day breakfast place in a 1940s style cafe, I had eggs benedict and a pot of tea. It was a lovely end to our time, it had been better than I'd thought considering so little organisation had gone on. We made the journey home, all knackered and somewhat quieter by this point.

I was still only doing about 2 hours each day at work, there seemed little point in increasing my hours when I was finishing anyway. I just went in and did what I could and came home and slept. On Thursday the 9th July, I was off to the Royal again, with dad as my chauffeur this time, for another stress test. As is always the case it took several attempts to get my bloods. Then off to get an ECG and dad off on his travels, back to ward 9B for me. I waited 20 mins or so to be given my medication then you just lie there and wait for it to take effect, but by 11.10 and I wasn't feeling symptomatic, normally I felt all hot and bothered, shaky and dizzy too; so I didn't think that I was where I should have been. My blood

147

sugar was 2.8 so I needed more medication, I do every time, but then it properly dropped to 1.9, the bloods later showed that at this point my blood sugar was actually only 1.2. Basically what the test is aiming to do is to make you hypoglycemic.

'Hypoglycemia, also known as low blood sugar, is when blood sugar decreases to below normal levels. This may result in a variety of symptoms including clumsiness, trouble talking, confusion, loss of consciousness, seizures or death. A feeling of hunger, sweating, shakiness, and weakness may also be present. Symptoms typically come on quickly.

I had a proper hypo, the worst I had ever had, I didn't know where I was, I felt awful, I couldn't move, it seemed to go on ages and then I must have passed out. When I came around the doctor was saying,

"Oh, you're back with us, are you?

I had a lucozade can to my mouth, which they had obviously been feeding me to get my blood sugar up more quickly, which I had never had needed before.

"Can you drink this yourself now?"

I felt like I'd had a bottle of wine, I was all disorientated, it took longer than normal to properly come around and I was so sticky, wet and cold from sweating. Then when the nurse went to take more bloods the cannula gave up and they had to try and get the blood out of somewhere else. It was the worst I'd felt after having the test and when I got home I needed a kip straight off but when my alarm went off after an hour and a half I was convinced it was morning and I didn't want to get up. I chilled for the remainder of the day as it had totally wiped me out.

That night, I wrote the following in my diary,

'Looking at my bloods and symptoms, side effects and getting the right balance and it just makes me think that this is going to be a long haul and getting it finely tuned will be an almost impossible task. I think it's really important that I know and understand what's going on because I see it all......I see so many docs and consultants but none look at the whole picture, knowing what's the NORM for me. So, I'll continue to learn and keep records so I can prove and point out when things need addressing. It also shows the docs I won't be fobbed off with a vague explanation and that I know what I'm talking about.'

The following morning, firstly I'd forgotten that the dog groomer was coming, so jumped up when she knocked and let her in in my pj's, I hate rushing about, it seems to throw me off somehow. I then when went to pick Tracey up before realising she'd already gotten a lift, I had a feeling that it was gonna be one of those days. Knackered at work so, I just worked slowly. I was going away in the van for the weekend, but when I tried to start it, it wouldn't start, that was my third and hopefully final thing going wrong! It was making all sorts of odd noises, but none of them the right ones. The man from the storage place saw me struggling and he sorted out a jumpstart by way of a bloody big John Deere tractor, it but it did the trick, I was so grateful to both men. I drove to Wrenbury, which is a bit windy with some narrow parts, but it was fine, I just took it slow and steady, because it was the first time I'd driven it down windy lanes and I arrived to a cheering crowd.

Then Harley, dad's friend from Spain, and dad took over and put water in the tank but when they turned the engine off it wouldn't start again. So, a new battery was needed. It was an Elvis weekend which my sister Tessa helped to organise, there was lots of people I knew there, so it was a good relaxed affair. Dad said to rest up but I couldn't with all the mess in the van, I made a start then Tes came to help and put most things away with me, which I was grateful for. It would need further thought and rejigging but I had made a start; I'd bought too much of some things and not enough of others. I had a nap, then before going out to the show, it was in the function room of the Cotton arms and we were parked up on the campsite which is behind, so it's a short walk there and back. First on were the Passionettes, two girl backing singers, who did a great ABBA tribute session. Then there was a 'younger' Elvis tribute on and I left as soon as he had finished, I needed my bed, the rest of my family stayed for the disco.

On the Saturday morning, I lay in bed wishing I had someone to make me a brew, my head and neck were aching and would hopefully ease once I got up. I did eventually and had a little tidying session and sorting before going around to

Tessa's caravan, we had lunch, then in the afternoon there's always a bit of a jamming session. Jack and Ella came up and Jack got up and sang a couple of songs and he went down really well, especially as he was not an Elvis artists! In the evening, the Passionettes did a Motown session and were as impressive as ever and then Paul, the main act came on and did his stint, he really is very good, one of the best around. His sets are always very entertaining too, he is just very comfortable on stage. The next morning, I was woken by the lawn mower mowing the field outside, then Kim and Ant turned up with the battery for my van and bless him Harley fitted it for me.

I was parked up next to Kathy and Harley who are seasoned travelers, so I was picking their brains again and Cathy asked why my feet and legs were painful and why I struggled walking, I didn't really have an answer. I didn't really know; I'd been told by several consultants that it wasn't directly caused by the tumour but that it was likely 'something else going on'. The only thing I could think, was that my body wasn't healing itself properly, as a result 'normal' wear and tear, aches and pains become exaggerated in my body. In the afternoon, we were back watching 'Elvis' again, it was the final session of the Elvis weekend, a Gospel session, which was very good again. As soon as it was finished at 3pm, I left for home.

I was definitely feeling the effects of my weekend away the following morning; when I'm that tired it's like my mind and body are on a go slow. I was on my way to work when I got a text off Tracey, then a call I missed .... I'd forgotten her. I thought that her hubby was bringing her, despite having a conversation the previous night to say I was picking her up, it must have been my tired brain! Work was alright, my heart really wasn't in it and the fatigue wasn't helping. When I had finished, I was straight home and back to bed, I could quite happily have stayed but I was due to meet up with Claire and Deb at Costa Coffee. It was a mini SSC meeting but it was still a great catch up. After, I nipped to see Lisa for an hour, I didn't want to let her down, so we caught up on the latest news. I had so much going on, friends to see, things planned in; I was determined to make the most of everything, even if it meant that for the rest of those days I was in bed!

Wednesday 15th, I had a call from the office that I needed to go and sort out my final paperwork; while I was in there two members of staff came in. I had only told a handful of people that I was leaving, but these two ladies I hadn't told, so I was a bit on edge that they would hear something. Luckily the conversation stopped until they had left and I was able to get signed up and sorted. When I got home I had a letter off the Open University, I ripped it open because I thought that it might be my degree grading; it was and I was absolutely over the moon to read that I had been given a 2.1, it was a relief that all of my hard work had actually paid off. It really did lift my spirits. I had another nap and when I woke feeling rough I decided that I wasn't going into work the next day, I needed to have a rest day and get myself sorted. I had been working every day, only for a couple of hours but I felt like I was forever playing catch up with myself.

On my day off I turned off my alarm and I slept until gone 10am but I still felt unwell, I felt sickie, very hot and sweaty, I really thought that I was going to be sick. I made myself a drink and I went back to lie down again and take some anti sickness medication to see if I felt any better. I spent the day mainly lying down because I felt better lying but not great standing. My cousin Carol came in the evening armed with flowers, we had a good catch up, bless, she had a lot on her plate because her parents weren't well and they lived two hours away and to add to her burden she had a teenage son! My two are grown up now and they have grown into amazing young adults, who can carry themselves well in any situation. People ask if my two were really difficult and stroppy when they were teens and I don't like to sound cocky but I really don't remember either of them being that bad, they both had their moments but honestly nothing significant. I'm not sure if I was lucky or they were well trained!

The next day I was at hospital again but locally this time, to hopefully get my nose sorted, it had been a problem since the operation and if anything, it had been getting worse not better. I had spoken with Mr. Sinha about the problems and he had referred me to get it checked out. I was seen by Dr. Dean, he put on this head lamp and he had a look up my nose and he said that I had, chronic atrophic rhinitis,

'Atrophic rhinitis is a chronic nasal condition with unknown cause. It is characterised by the formation of thick dry crusts in a roomy nasal cavity, which has resulted from progressive wasting away or decrease in size of the mucous nasal lining and underlying bone'

He then proceeded to spray some anesthetic up my nose and then I had to sit for another 5 mins for it to work. I

153

was called back in and he got out his strange head light gear and suckered and plucked and proceeded to basically pick my nose, it was soooo gross and it bloody hurt too; I didn't look at what he removed but it confirmed his diagnosis anyway. He instructed me to use the nasal rinse stuff 4 times a day (he said 6 originally!!) And he'd see me in a month, to check that it was doing the trick of healing my nose. Reading about it was more serious than I'd appreciated as it can corrode the insides of your nose and also cause more general health issues too, including TIREDNESS would you believe?!

The next day, we were going to do some shopping, partially for the cruise but mainly for the wedding which we had coming up. The kids were slow to rouse, neither wanting to move from their bed, Ella more than Jack; Tes was coming and driving us. We set off to Chester with the kids moaning and threatening to be sick in the back of the car, we arrived about 11.20. We went straight to the hungry horse for some breakfast, it was lovely and perked the kids up a bit too. I took my wheelchair as my back had been killing me on top of everything else and I'd got no energy at all; so at least in my wheelchair I was less of a hindrance. First off, we got Jack sorted with a new suit in the sale at £60, it was a bit different, blue with a little check; we also got him a couple of pairs of smart trousers and a jacket, so he just needed some shirts, ties and shoes and he'd be set. Ella got all sorted in Coast; one fabulous gown at £110!! It looked stunning on though. Jack couldn't wait to get done but with Ella she's posing and taking pictures and loving the whole thing. I managed one buy and that was because it was next to me while I was parked up in my wheelchair, it was a long jacket, patterned and sheer, it would go over my clothes cover me up! By this time, we'd ran out of steam so we called in at Costa but we were all past recharging, I knew I was tired because my body was jerking. It was a quieter journey on the way home because we had called at KFC and so the kids were occupied eating, once home we all went off for a sleep!

The next morning, I was up and ready in plenty of time but when I went to start my car the battery was totally dead, luckily Ella was off, so she gave me and Tracy a lift to work. I just hoped that it was a simple jump start and not something bigger going on, cars are great but when they go wrong they are blinkin expensive luxuries. It was the day before the school finished for Summer, so I went and told Steve and Helen, who now ran my former unit, about me going. I think that it was a bit of a shock to them, but the truth was because I had missed so much time from work I didn't know the new staff, so there was only so many who would know who I was and fewer still who would miss me. When I got home I had to sort out my car, I got green flag out and they said that the battery had gone; luckily, I had my receipt for it and it was only fitted 18 months ago and luckily, it had a 2-year warranty. So, it meant that I could get a new one for free, perfect! I had a call off the Royal asking if I could attend an appointment with the endocrine doctor, the following Tuesday, so hopefully I'd get some answers.

The 21st of July, was my last day at school, I was feeling weird about it, as so few people knew and that's fine but it makes the situation odd. I wanted it, I needed it, however, it was a little exciting and scary in equal measure, looking forward to the next steps in my life. I faffed until concert time, which I thoroughly enjoyed, it's always good to celebrate student's achievements and to showcase their skills and talent. Then at the end of the concert, Jason, the headmaster, got all the staff leaving ,up on stage!! I could see some people's shocked faces and when I came off the stage several people came up to me and wished me luck and gave me a hug. There were quite a few people leaving - I'd said that I didn't want a fuss so Jason just did a short dedication, other dedications were sad, some were funny. But for me it was the end of an era and hopefully the start of a new phase for me, after a couple of months doing nothing!

I had started with a headache which was a rarity for me, so I went up to bed at 9.30 and took some morphine, but I couldn't settle, I just lay there thinking about what a momentous day it had been for me. The kids kept joking saying 'what's it like being on the dole?', but the reality was that I may never have a conventional 9-5 job again. I didn't know what my future work life would be but I wanted to see if I could do something online with my group work and maybe some consultancy work. I had been thinking about it because it would be something that I could do without physically taxing myself too much, then once it was set up; I wanted to get writing my book, while things were still relatively clear in my mind. I'm sure that it would be beneficial to sufferers, relatives and friends, plus I thought that I'd find it therapeutic too. I was lucky that I had choices; do I keep the house or sell it, I had cash in the bank for the first time ever I think, so I was pretty set for a while if I was careful. I wrote this in my diary,

'I've got so many true and loyal friends that I can't fit them all in lol. My overwhelming feeling tonight is one of thankfulness. There's many hurdles yet to cross but there's going to be some good shit in between!!'

Chapter 13

The DVLA!!

Wednesday 22nd July and I was off to Uttoxeter to meet up with mum, dad, Tes and Macy for a few days away and watching the horse racing too. I was getting more and more confident driving my van and I actually enjoyed driving it, because you sit quite high, you can see more ahead and it was a pleasure to drive. Once I got there I hooked up the electrics and I had a bit of a sort out but by 3pm I was in need of a nap and I slept till 5, it was fine naps are acceptable when you're on holiday! I went around to Tessa's van where everyone was staying and we had a Chinese takeaway and lots of talking. When I went back to the van and got ready for bed I found a lump on my instep, I'd had a reflexology session a couple of days before and I wondered if it was that, I asked my reflexologist, Trina, and she said that she didn't think so but the area where it was, was associated with my bladder. I find it fascinating that when you have reflexology, they can tell you so much about your body, normally I hate having my feet touched; when the kids want to torture me, they will try and tickle my feet, but for some reason I love having reflexology.

The following day I had planned to do some sewing and get the old-fashioned cushion covers in my van taken off and new ones made, Tes came to help me, it was a fairly straight forward task actually, the hardest part was getting the big cushion pads back in the covers again. By the end of the day they were all done and I was knackered but happy with the results. We went out for tea and then I came straight back to the van and began watching a programme where people marry before they ever meet their spouse, it was the most bizarre thing, I kept thinking 'good god if I had had to marry some of my first dates', oooooohhhhh noooooo, the thought of it made me shudder. Why would someone sign up to such a programme? The next day, I sewed the curtains for the van in the morning and there were races in the afternoon, Tes always collects our bets and walks and puts them on for us, she never moans she just gets on with it. Jack had driven up to join us which was nice and he had brought our dog, Charlie with him too. By the end of the racing I had somehow managed to be £40 up, I only ever look at the name so it was just random good luck! I never even went outside to cheer them on either, I just sat inside and chilled.

On the Saturday, I didn't wake until 10am and I had had 5 texts off Ella, she text, that she was on her way but because it was so late she was already there. I did some more sewing and sorted out bits and bobs and organised things, it was beginning to feel more like home, more comfy and cozy, I was really happy with the transformation. We all ended up at Tessa's to eat tea, as there was more room in her caravan. Then we played the 'Bobby Charlton game'; it's known by different names but this is how we play it, it always starts with Bobby Charlton, hence the name, and then the next person has to think of a name beginning with C, say Charles Bronson and so on, it can keep us occupied for hours!!

The following day, there was racing again and there was a One Direction tribute band on, so Tes and the kids went over to see what was going on and I stayed back and had a sleep. Unfortunately, the weather was awful, it was raining really heavily, poor Tes got soaked running back and forth, I didn't do quite so well on the races but I was still £15 up, which wasn't so bad at all. It is always mad and noisy when we all get together, so it was a great day but I was ready for some peace and quiet at the end of it all. Me, Jack and Ella went back to our van in the evening and had food and watched a film. Jack however, is the clumsiest person I have ever met, we call him Jack OOPs Gray! He nearly tipped up the table three times, on the forth he managed to do it and blackcurrant juice went all over my lovely new cream covers, as luck would have it, I had sprayed the covers with a stain repellant spray so the juice just sat on the top rather than soaking in and stain the new covers.

Then next day, the kids were off home, I had yet another two hour nap, tea at Tessa's and then another early night. The following day, Tuesday 28th, I had an appointment at the Royal in Liverpool, dad took me, I was seeing the endocrinologist Dr. Sharma. We discussed how things were going, he told me that I had to continue with my hydrocortisone, because the tests had showed that I needed it, and the likelihood was that I would need to take it for the rest of my life. The other concern was that my blood results seemed to show that I had some sort of issue with my kidneys, I had been concerned about them too, so he suggested that I have two 24-hour urine tests, as these would give a better picture of how my kidneys were functioning. So, I came away with two containers for my tests and instructions of what to do.

The next day we packed up, it literally takes me about 5 minutes to do, so I packed up and was off quite quickly. I'd had such a lovely time, I'd got lots of things done, I'd had a lovely relaxing time so I went home with a smile on my face. Then I got home opened my mail for the week and I had a letter off the DVLA,

'We have received medical information as part of this enquiry telling us that you have a brain tumour, so you must not drive for 6 months from completion of your treatment. This period is to ensure the risk of having an epileptic seizure falls to a level acceptable for ordinary driving and to ensure a satisfactory response to any treatment given.

This means that your entitlement to drive will be revoked from 28/7/15.'

I was livid because;

1. I had told them of my brain tumour 2 years before.

2. Where my tumour was didn't trigger seizures.

3. I had driven back with no licence!

What the heck was that all about? I had informed the DVLA that I had had my operation about a month or so before, I had detailed what operation I had had and that I'd had the all clear to drive from my surgeon. When I looked at the DVLA's own guidance on limitations on driving, like you couldn't drive for a year after an epileptic seizure for example; when I checked what it was for my operation, it said that I could drive straight away and for radiation it was at the most a one-month recovery period. So, I should have been fine to drive. When I called the DVLA, I stupidly assumed that they would just say 'oh yes, we've made a mistake', but nooooo not a chance. They just wouldn't listen to what I had to say, they kept saying we will need to investigate it. So, my driving license was revoked until they investigated!!!! I couldn't believe it just when things seemed to be falling into place, I had the rug pulled from under me again, I was furious.

You don't realise how isolating it can be not being able to drive until you experience it, it takes away your independence; the bus stop was too far for me to walk to and there was no seat there, so catching a bus was out of the question. I just couldn't believe that they could be so stubborn and thoughtless, plus, the holiday with Joanna in the van we couldn't do either, because I couldn't drive. By the end of the week though, we had booked an all-inclusive week abroad to Mallorca; I was happy that I would be flying short haul and seeing how the tumour responded, before I had to do the long-haul flight for the cruise. After the tumour had bled, which prompted the need for my operation, I was concerned that when I flew again, it could maybe cause another issue, Mr. Sinha had said that he thought that it would be fine but there was still a niggling doubt for me. My spirits were lifted somewhat by my friend Tracey, who had gotten married since I had seen her last, she brought her wedding pictures to show me. They were amazing and so many unique and funny ones, pictures and videos are so great at capturing memories which you can later look back on. Then Ella's friend, Katie came to cook for us, she is a great little cook and so we were treated to a lovely meal, which I hadn't had to do myself. Plus, we all had a moan about the stupid DVLA!! I'd already sent an email to my surgeon telling him and a letter to see if that would sort the issue out, but I just had to wait and it was frustrating.

On the Saturday, I was out with the hens again, just locally but again I prepared in my normal manner; I got up late, I did little all day and I had another nap in the afternoon, plus I took an extra 5 mg of hydrocortisone to give me a boost too. I had bought a black and white jumpsuit for the occasion, and I felt ok and I planned to stay out as long as I could. Me and Joanna, met up with all the other hens, plus some who hadn't been on the weekend away; we had the obligatory cocktails, plus a shot too, I thought crikey if we carry on like this I'll be back and in bed in no time. We called at a couple of bars, the others tended to dance while I found a chair to sit on, to watch and do a little sit-down dancing. At the end of the night we ended up in bar which stayed open later, I had my reservations but I went with the flow. I knew that I would know some people in there, the trouble was that the chances were that they would be the kid's friends and former pupils who I had worked with. Both Jack and Ella were in there with their friends, then two young men came over, Nathan and Cohen, they were boys who I had worked with, while they were at school. It was lovely that they had come over rather than do their best to avoid me and they both spoke about how they were at school and thanked me for being there for them, which is so rewarding. It was another reminder that I would truly miss working with young people. Jack had been due to take me home but he had had a drink so Ella walked me out to the taxi rank and made sure that I was ok, it was 1 am so I thought that I had done very well.

The following day was definitely a pyjama day, we all lazed around doing very little. Then in the afternoon I had a telephone call,

"Hello this Cheshire police, we have had a call saying that your car is blocking number 2 Langdon drive."

"Ok......"

"The car is registered to Mr. Jack Gray, can we please speak with him."

So, I covered the phone and shouted up to Jack,

"Jack, the police are on the phone."

"Yeah right, good one!!"

"No really Jack it's the police."

So he came running down the stairs with a worried look on his face, the police officer was obviously asking him questions but I could only hear Jack's responses.

"It's parked on the front of my house!"

The he looked out of the window,

"No it's not there, I think it's been stolen!"

"Do you think that you might have left the handbrake on?" the police lady asked.

Jack ran out the front and his car indeed on the lawn of number 2 Langdon! It turned out that he had left his handbrake off and his car had rolled about 20 feet but it had been stopped by a huge bag of sand on the lawn of the house two doors down!! He was lucky that there hadn't been any other cars in the way and his was undamaged. He knocked on the door of the house and no one answered. The man at the house, which turned out to be 2 Langdon, had called the police, instead of coming and knocking on our door, Jack OOPs Gray, strikes again!

I did my first 24-hour urine sample collection, I had two, 2 litre containers for the two tests but by the time that I had finished the test I had almost filled both of the containers; bless her, Tes took them to the doctors for me disguised in bags. The following day the doctor's surgery telephoned saying that I had another water infection and that I needed another course of antibiotics, plus I had to see the doctor for yet another check-up. I was concerned about my kidney's, so I made a call to Dr. Sharma's secretary, the hormone guy, she said that she would chase up my results and also that I was being referred to a specialist a Dr. Shultz, so I was just waiting for an appointment and a scan on my kidneys which would hopefully show what was happening.

The following evening, I met up with Elaine and one of my best friends growing up, Diane; we had lost touch a little so it was lovely meeting up and reminiscing together and catching up with how all our lives were going. In the week, I also met up with Lisa who had finished at work, Tes dropped us off and we had a lovely afternoon tea and a couple of cocktails; lots of talk about impending holidays, Lia's' wedding and how glad she was to be off for a few weeks. Saturday the 8th August, I was going on the train to see my hospital friend, Sheila, Tes dropped me at the station and Sheila picked me up the other end. We spent hours drinking tea and putting the world to rights, we see so many things the same way, it's a tonic. Her friend Donna who I'd met at Sheila's birthday bash, popped round; she fit in perfectly because she'd survived breast cancer and a divorce too. I stayed over and the next morning we had more brews and more talking; Sheila was struggling at work and was negotiating finishing but she still had doubts so we talked through her concerns and she seemed to feel better about it all. It is such a big step in many ways, because it affects your identity, so many people ask 'Oh what do you do for a living?' When you don't work you can feel less fulfilled, especially if illness is the reason that you have finished.

On a daily basis I was still struggling, everything seemed to hurt, I was still sleeping at least 11 hours at night plus the odd nap too and each week I seemed to have a new symptom or problem; so I needed some things to plan in so that I had a different, more positive focus. I was somewhat nervous about going away because I wouldn't have the safety blanket of knowing that I had a hospital 5 minutes away and the specialist brain hospital only an hour away. I did need to get my head around it though because I had trips already organised; a week with Joanna, a trip with Mum and dad, my cruise and next year I planned to be away for a month at a time!! There was lots planned in-between and it was an exciting time. I got my travel insurance sorted; I struggled to

166

get comparisons because no one would insure me, so I was running out of options. In the end I had two quotes, one for £1000, I chose one with good cover for £650 (for a year worldwide cover) plus it included 'companion ' cover for an extra £10! So, I included that which made the whole deal seem far better.

I had to rely on other people again because I couldn't drive so Joanna took me to the dentist for a check-up and then we went to Frankie and Benny's for brunch, I love it there. I had done very little for a few days however, I was still knackered but at least I didn't have anything pressing that I had to do. I was happy being out, I was not liking not being able to drive, it is so isolating. Friday the 14th was the wedding of Joanna's brother Stuart, it was at magnificent local place called Haslington Hall. It was a perfect wedding day apart from the dodgy weather, it was August and the weather was like flippin Winter. The food was delicious, the speeches emotional and the outfits varied. I had even managed to have an afternoon nap, in Joanna's room because we weren't staying over, unfortunately, I had missed most of Jack's set because he had been asked to sing. In the evening, the DJ was exceptional the dance floor was full all night, I had a couple of dances and the rest of the time I videoed the dancing and I got some great and funny clips. It really was a fantastic day, I do love a good wedding.

The next day was another pyjama day, Joanna popped for a debrief. Then Elaine who had yet again had Charlie for us popped round with him. When Charlie goes to Elaine's he is spoilt, he is fed chicken and Elaine's three children; George, Ben and Maddie make a big fuss of him and they love to walk him too, so as you can imagine it's like a holiday home for Charlie, he loves it. However, he'd given Elaine quite a fright, he'd gone exploring and got stuck, so when Elaine called him he didn't come, they checked the neighbours' gardens and the street but no Charlie. Then as they were exploring their own garden again, they heard him crying, he'd gone routing and got stuck in the bushes; Shaun, Elaine's husband, had to cut him out, they've since cut it all down in case he gets stuck again! We ordered a Chinese takeaway for tea and we always order too much, so I plate it up for another meal or two for the next day. However, I'd been up in my room and when I came down for a drink I found that Jack had eaten the extra food! He's such a greedy so and so, if we have goodies in, I have to divide it up otherwise I wouldn't get a look in; I have to cut cakes up and assign pieces, I even write names on cereal boxes. It's like a military operation feeding Jack and I don't think he has ever been full. He's always starving, not hungry, starving!

The Monday, I was back at the doctors for more blood tests, then onto my local hospital for a follow up appointment with Dr. Dean in the 'Ear, Nose and throat' department. He examined my nose and confirmed that although he had been concerned about my 'chronic atrophic rhinitis', he said that it was much improved. I had to continue my nasal rinses with the solution, I still have to do them, plus I sneeze far more than normal because I have no hairs up my nose like you normally do. My mum and dad had taken me and when they dropped me off I had a nap, I was struggling to get through most days without one, but I forgot to set my alarm and I ended up sleeping for 2.5 hours. A call from the doctors actually woke me, they said that I had another infection and they had more antibiotics for me, I'd lost count of how many I'd had, plus I had to an extra 10 mg hydrocortisone while I was on them too.

On Tuesday 18th, I went away with Joanna again, dad took us to the airport and after travelling for several hours we arrived at our hotel, late at night. The hotel was lovely, our room was clean and the food was gorgeous, plus there was no fighting for sunbeds which is a distinct benefit, I will not get up early on holiday just to get a sunbed. The first couple of days were pretty uneventful, just pool, lunch, a top up of sun-cream, then the pool again, then back to the room, shower and a nap before going back out. On the Thursday, we decided to take the short walk to the beach, it was beautiful with a harbour and plenty to see, we paid 16 euros for the beds but better than sand everywhere. We lasted until 2.30 then we traipsed back, we nipped to our room, before going down back down to the pool. Back in the room I showered and slathered myself in aloe vera, ready for a kip. We had a nice meal and sat in the bar playing cards, then this creepy French guy came over and sat with us, he kept touching Joanna and talking nonsense, I found it a little amusing because I was a safe distance away!

When we went down to the pool the following morning, we couldn't decide on our position, because there was shade which moved around certain sections; in the end, we chose a spot in the sunny area, then Joanna spotted a lone towel,

"OMG, I hope that's not the creepy guys towels from last night."

So, just in case, we moved to the opposite end and put our towels out, but by the time we'd gone and put cream on and come back down the lone towel was right next to Joanna's with the FRENCH MAN on it. I had to stifle a laugh, Joanna did her best not to make eye contact for fear of giving him the green light. He moved after about an hour or so but it was funny, what are the odds? When we went in for lunch we asked the reception about keeping our room on our last day and we also spoke to them about the noise last night in the room next to us. Then we were nervous going back to the room and back again in case we ran into the noisy people from last night, we didn't know what they looked like but we knew what they sounded like. The following day we'd both had enough of the sun by 5pm, so we made an early retreat to our room. I'd got a headache, so I only a little to eat but no alcohol and my head eased, we sat outside and it was lovely and chilled. We'd been back in our room a while when there was more mayhem from outside the room; screaming, crying and shouting but not from next door this time, you'd have thought that we were in an 18-30 hotel!

We'd both taken 'Gone girl' to read, we were reading it for our book-club and it was getting entertaining, Joanna would 'ooohh' and I'd say what bit are you up to? And vice versa and we were playing detective, with figuring out who was guilty in the book and trying to figure out who the people involved last night were. Later in the afternoon we walked to the front, it wasn't that far but my feet were killing me, we were going to walk along a bit but it was too hot and the sea was rough, so we just had a paddle then watched the world go, we were entertained by some very nice bodies about. We had a gorgeous ice-cream well mine was sorbet, it was lovely and cooling. Then all of a sudden, I needed the TOILET!! I honestly thought I'd have a nasty accident on the way back, I was walking as fast as my stupid legs would carry me, luckily, I made it just in time. I had a shower but I knew that my legs were going to kill from walking too fast to get back and my feet were killing me too, but better than an accident!

On our last day we spent it in the sun and despite not being able to keep our room we another one, so we were able to shower before being picked up. It was only a short trip to the airport, then a queue to book in, but on the plus side we got rid of our hand luggage too. Subway for tea and no alcohol needed for Joanna to board the plane, she'd got her wing, I'd seen a different side to her that holiday; she liked watching 'you've been framed' especially the ones where it looks like someone gets hurt, the phrase 'die' was used on more than one occasion, plus apparently, she sees and hears EVERYTHING! It had been another great break full of fun and laughter and the odd strange Frenchman.

At Manchester airport, we were quickly through and dad picked us up again. We were about half way home and I asked if he had my front door key, because I had left it in the well of his car,

"Oh, I think Kim borrowed it."

"Why did Kim need it?"

"I don't know."

"How am I going to get in now?"

It was nearly midnight and I had no key, I was tired and niggly and I was not happy. I had to get in touch with Jack and he stayed up to let me in. Then to add insult to injury I quickly checked my mail before I went bed and I saw one from the DVLA, I got a little excited but it was merely acknowledging receipt of my letter, but not saying that I could drive!!!

Chapter 14

Away with the folks

On Sundays, I treated myself to a lie in, so I don't have my alarm on, on that Sunday I didn't actually wake up until after 11am, soon after Ella did her usual 'let's go the pheasant'....... it's a place that she loves to eat at, it's a 30-minute drive but it does have gorgeous food and wonderful views of the Cheshire countryside. So, I thought why not, Ella was driving all I had to do was sit there and eat, so we got ready and traipsed off, we only got lost a little which was usual. We had a lovely pork roast dinner each and then we called at the ice-cream farm, it had had a major makeover and as a result was really busy and the queues were too long so we didn't get any!! We had a good talk about boys, work, holidays and where I was up to with kidney situation; Ella seems to be able to handle it, the whole truth, which I don't discuss with others because it's all a bit much for most to cope with, I just hoped she doesn't go away and mull over things too much.

I didn't do a lot the next few days, I had an hour's blast, doing some tidying up and cleaning, which was all that I could manage, but something is better than nothing I suppose. I felt that my fatigue wasn't getting any better; if I rested up I stiffened and still had no energy, if I forced myself to try and do things it seemed the same, so I thought it seemed better to do things than just sit there, so that's what I did. I was getting frustrated at not being able to get things done; I still wasn't adjusting to my 'new' life very well. I was lucky that I had time, I wasn't working so I should have been able to make adjustments but unfortunately I always wanted more; energy, strength and stamina!

On the 1st of September, Deb called about for a catch up, she'd been away in her caravan in the UK and she look really well, browner than me by far. Lisa arrived just before 5pm and we caught up on our respective holidays and adventures over the Summer. When she left, I began to feel weird, I was having a funny do, a sugar low, I then realised that I'd not eaten all day, so I had some orange juice and took my hydrocortisone despite it being too late really, then I sat quietly while it all took effect. Later that afternoon my friend Tridge, arrived with half the pups from her dog's litter in her car, to show me bless her, her dog had had 16 puppies so she had had to help feed them, she'd been up all hours and working too. I love her I can be honest and she's ok with that - I said I felt crappy she said,

"I'm not gonna lie, you don't look great!"

She was right, I didn't.

The following day, I had to take took my van for a 'habitation check', dad driving, me directing. I wanted to make sure that everything inside was in good working order and safe for when we began our travels. Ella and I had talked some more and we had more or less decided that we would do a month away at a time, with a month in-between for me to fit in all my hospital appointments and for Ella to work. We'd also discussed where we might go to and we thought that Spain would be a good first choice because we could stop off where mum and dad were and pick up some tips while we visited them. We had also talked about Italy, France, Germany and Ireland, but we weren't planning too far ahead but at some point in the future we would need to pencil in possible dates because of hospital appoints and the like.

Jack's birthday is the 3rd September and we had decided to go for food once Ella was home from work, but trying to sort going somewhere for tea was like pulling teeth but we ended up at the Cat it was nice but funny because Jack was as ever STARVING and his meal was by far the smallest. I wasn't the best company I felt out of sorts, exhausted and just no patience; on the way home Ellie Goulding's HOW WILL I LOVE THEE came on and I teared up, I was just having an emotional moment!! I got some bits sorted for when I was away and I left Tes with a list of tasks to do while I was away and within an hour she'd done most things on the list. Also, I spoke to another muppet at the DVLA, useless, jobs worth, plonkers; it was just so frustrating because they were trying to say they still had further investigations to do despite my conditions not warranting any revoking of my license. Tes was going to see what she could do!!

On the 5th, I was going away with my mum and dad for a trip through Belgium following my grandad's steps during the second world war. Dad called to say they were leaving whilst I was still in bed!! Quick shower and change luckily, I had sorted my stuff. We loaded up finally got off about 11, then we got stuck in traffic on the M6 - if we'd have gone on the toll we'd have been ok, we arrived about 2pm to friends of mum and dads, Brian and Wendy. We arrived to a laid table and a 3-course meal which was lovely. Brian had a tour of my van and I had a tour of their grounds and their van; they had a beautiful place. Brian and Wendy had been invited out and because we contacted them last minute about going they couldn't let their friends down, me and dad sat down to watch the launch of strictly, I love it; mum had been faffing somewhere so when she came in and sat down, I set her up. Dad had his feet up on the recliner part of the sofa, so I said to mum,

"Why don't you put yours up?"

"Oh noooooooo."

She pooh, poohed it. I said,

"Just push back, it will be more comfortable."

Then she did and she was pushing like mad and nothing was happening, me and dad held it together for a short time and then doubled up laughing, because her chair didn't actually go back! Moments like that are little bits of happiness! The following morning, we had a quick breakfast and said our goodbyes. We made pretty good time and arrived and checked in by 12.30, while we waited to go on the boat we made a lunch to take on board; we soon found some seats and tucked into our picnic. I then promptly lay back and fell asleep till we arrived!

Once off the boat, we followed directions from an OFFLINE app which I had uploaded the destinations on, so that I didn't have to use lots of data trying not to get lost. I'd done lots of pre-planning it had given me something to do;

finding out about each destination, deciding on our route, researching where would be best to stop and how we could get about once we were there. I am ok to alter the route and destinations but I like to plan because then you don't miss something which might be just a few miles off route. Our first stop off was in a small campsite just on the edge of the town of DE ZWERVER BRUGSESTEENWEG NIEUWPOORT, it was just a pit stop on our way really. We couldn't figure out the showers and how to pay but a nice Dutch lady helped us out. I wanted to try these sorts of camp stops to see if they're worth it or not as a test for when I travelled with Ella.

Dad had a quick shower and we then walked a short distance into the town, there were lots of restaurants but they were quite expensive, we ended up in a Chinese. Almost immediately I felt weird, I was having a funny do, it came on really quickly, normally I had extra medication and a sweet snack in my handbag but I hadn't brought it out, it was just typical. Mum rushed to some nearby shops for some sweet stuff; whilst she was gone dad asked the waiter for a biscuit. I felt awful, I go all dizzy and shaky and I can't talk properly and even once I've eaten something, it takes a few minutes to take effect, after about 15 minutes I felt a lot better, but I didn't eat much food, it always shakes me up a bit.

The next day we followed directions via offline maps which was pretty good again and we arrived in BRUGES about 12.30; the site was a basic car park type layout, with electric but little else. It was ideally positioned on the edge of the City, we got a bus into the centre.

'If you set out to design a fairy-tale medieval town, it would be hard to improve on central Bruges (Brugge in Dutch). Picturesque cobbled lanes and dreamy canals link photogenic market squares lined with soaring towers, historic churches and old whitewashed alms-houses. And there's plenty of it.'

We found a lovely restaurant; dad had mussels and then half a roast chicken, me and mum had a 3- course meal offer; soup, Flemish stew and chocolate mousse. Once refueled, we had a wander around, it really is a beautiful place, lovely buildings and architecture with some very old parts and dates on lots of buildings. We made our way back, calling at a little cafe for hot chocolate which was amazing, the final part of the walk though not far was hard for all of us; my feet really hurt, my legs, my shoulders and my back always the same I don't know why. I was knackered so I got into my pj's by 6.30 and was up on my bed and had 40 winks. I was woken by an alarm going off, some women in a nearby van nearly had an accident with their gas, some connection seemed to have come off, it made an awful noise of escaping gas, then 10 minutes later one of them was smoking!!

The next day was another slow morning, we didn't set off until 11.30, we made our way down some little streets and lanes to OOSTKAPELLE, isn't that such a fantastic name? Mum and dad had friends there who they hadn't seen for about 10 years, so we were calling in to see them; dad called Jan and Corrie and they gave us directions to their house and somehow we managed to find it on the map. We had a lovely lunch and catch up with them; Jan is fascinating, he's done so much and had so many different experiences and his English is brilliant because he was sent to England after the war for four years. After we moved on to our campsite ROOM PORT CAMPERLAND, it was a nice day so we sat outside soaking up some sun and having a wine.

We were off before 10am the following day and mum was stressing because I'd said to her I've hardly had any sleep, you'll need to take a turn in the front! It took longer to get to the HOOK OF HOLLAND than we had anticipated, but we travelled along some amazing roads, over lots of water, dams and water controls; I took lots of pictures which mainly turned out rubbish. Then we were following Hook of Holland signs and suddenly they were all crossed out on the signs but we didn't know what to do other than follow them; turns out there's a new bypass LUCY (our sat nav) knew nothing about. We figured it out, eventually. We followed a scenic route round, stopping at a café on the harbour watching the ships go by at the spot where we reckon my grandad would have been. He was on a ship which came to rescue the Queen of the Netherlands, as the German's advanced during the second world and the British army was retreating.

'On 10 May 1940, Germany invaded the Netherlands. There is an ongoing debate about the departure of the Queen and the royal family. Some say that an evacuation to the United Kingdom of the royal family had been planned some time in advance, since at least the end of 1939. Wilhelmina and her family fled The Hague, and she boarded HMS Herewald, a British destroyer which was to take her across the North Sea to England.'

There's nothing there to mark the event and we had to do a bit of digging to get to the bottom of where my grandad had been, but it was good to be there. Next we made our way to AMSTERDAM, mum and dad had never been I had been for Tessa's hen do years before.

'Amsterdam is the Netherlands' capital, known for its artistic heritage, elaborate canal system and narrow houses with gabled facades, legacies of the city's 17th-century Golden Age. Its Museum District houses the Van Gogh Museum, works by Rembrandt and Vermeer at the Rijksmuseum, and modern art at the Stedelijk. Cycling is key to the city's character, and there are numerous bike paths. Plus of course it's red light district!"

We managed to find the campsite with little difficulty, as it was pretty well signposted, plus the offline maps app was pretty impressive considering it was free. On arrival, there were a lot of youngsters, about, hippie types, and people who you would imagine would say 'Hey man' but when we booked in they were very efficient and helpful. We'd spoken about just booking one night and seeing how we went but as they were almost fully booked we booked for the two and she said if we changed our mind we could get a refund. By this time, it was 4ish, we set up and settled in, had a brew and then we all had naps! When I woke from mine I didn't want to go out so I stayed in and watched a film while mum and dad went out for food, they said it was very nice. All of the facilities were really good, it was a well thought out site, it even had an outdoor kitchen for campers to use and a huge herb garden.

The next day, we walked a short distance to catch the tram and I tried to note down where we were so we could get our bearings and not get lost. Amsterdam has lovely buildings, an intricate canal system and hundreds of bikes who assumed priority everywhere; it just had a lovely feel to the place. We started at Dam square and headed towards the station to get a canal cruise, we stopped and had hot drinks, gorgeous hot chocolate and cream for me and mum, dad a little coffee. When I took pictures, there was a sex museum sign above my mum and dad, it really titled me because they were oblivious. We didn't get the cruise we'd originally planned as there was one literally across the road and as we're all physically challenged, we decided on one of them. It was a good hour long and nice and chilled; it was great to see a different side to Amsterdam, all the history was explained too, which was fascinating, you always learn something on one of those types of tours. After we walked on the fringes of the red-light district but it was far calmer in the day than night, there were still some ladies in windows though; we were walking down a little alley way and we looked to the side and there was a naked woman sat in the window, which did make us all laugh.

Next we grabbed food from the street vendors and we made our way back to the Dam square where we jumped on the tram and got off to have a look around the flower market, where I bought some TULIPS FROM AMSTERDAM!! We got back on the tram and we got off earlier than we'd planned at Rembrandt Plein; which is a lovely square with a statue, a grass area, with cafes and bars around the edge, it looked beautiful so we got off and I had a lovely lemon infused bier. We got back on the tram to the end of the line and walked the short distance back to the camp, it was still warm (it had been

181

a gorgeous day) so I sat outside with a cider and caught up on some reading. In the evening, we went to the restaurant for food, it was very nice, I had the special which was mussels and linguine, very tasty too.

Friday 12th, the sun was shining and we were traveling about 2.20 hours to get to our next destination of GHENT,

'Ghent is a port city in northwest Belgium, at the confluence of the Leie and Scheldt rivers. During the Middle Ages it was a prominent city-state. Today it's a university town and cultural hub. Its pedestrianized center is known for medieval architecture such as 12th-century Gravensteen castle and the Graslei, a row of guildhalls beside the Leie river harbor.'

We stopped at a petrol station on the outskirts of Ghent to ask for directions and after a little diversion, we found the site; it was very good with spacious plots, but there was a funny smell coming from somewhere but great WIFI, you can't have everything! We had some food sat outside in the sun, chilled a little then set off for town about 4.30pm. We walked the short distance to the bus stop and got on the bus; there were lots of high rises on the outskirts but it had a very old historic centre. We had a little walk and ended up in a little bar by the castle, which was an imposing presence in the town. We then had another wander and we found somewhere to eat, De Kuip Van; it was set back from a large pedestrian area which served as a thoroughfare further into the town, so it was perfect for people watching. Mum and dad had mussels and I had chicken, plus we had some beers too, it is true what they say that you get the best beers in Belgium. It was really busy, we had a young Irish waiter serving us, who was very helpful and chatty and he gave us some tips on where else to go to eat and drink. It was going dark as we made our way back, it was nice seeing Ghent at night, because places look so different at night time when all the lights come on.

The next day, I took my crutch out, I'd not used it all the time but my legs weren't working well, it's like they forget what they are supposed to be doing, that's the only way I can describe it! We walked around the different parts of Ghent which were equally as spectacular as the night before and we saw a cast rehearsing West Side Story numbers for a show that night, they were brilliant and we sat and watched them for a good while, enjoying the free show. We stopped for hot drinks at a bar that Danny had recommended, for beer I think but it was a nice place overlooking water. Across the road was a stall selling different types of meat so we got chicken and potatoes for tea, then we bought fruit from a nearby shop, a proper greengrocers. We had lunch in a little café, soup and sandwiches and drinks all home-made and it was a well-earned pit stop.

Then I decided to go up Ghent belfry which reportedly had fantastic views over the city, it was a church belfry; luckily it had a lift, BUT there were also stairs, circular and awkward passing both ways, I was just told that there were a few stairs! Basically, you got to the top no problem and the view was by way of a balcony all around the top of the tower, you went one way around because there was no room to do otherwise, then you had to go down narrow twisty stairs. I got to the top and it wasn't as impressive as I'd imagined and it was a really tight squeeze, which I wasn't a fan of, then going down the narrowest of staircases frightened me, I thought I might get stranded. Even with good legs I'd have struggled, down those stairs, but with a crutch it was almost impossible because for some reason there was people coming up too! When I got out, mum and dad were sat watching another musical performance,

"How was it?"

"It was a good job that you pair didn't do it, I thought that I was going to get stuck at one point!"

We got the bus back but didn't pay somehow, rebels that we were!! Back at the van and I had another nap, once I woke we had food at the van and watched 'THE BLIND SIDE', it is an amazing true story and it made me cry again, despite having watched it many times before.

On the Sunday, we made our way towards YPRES,

'Ypres (leper), is a town in the Belgian province of West Flanders. It's surrounded by the Ypres Salient battlefields, where many cemeteries, memorials and war museums honor the battles that unfolded in this area during World War I. After being destroyed in the war, many important buildings were carefully reconstructed, including Gothic-style Sint-Maartens kathedraal (St. Martin's Cathedral) and its soaring spire.'

Dad wanted to avoid the motorways and I couldn't argue, we had originally been going to share the driving but my not being able to drive had put a spanner in the works; so, we had a scenic, whirly, longer route as a result. We stopped off briefly at Passendale museum but we didn't look around as it was too much walking, our legs weren't great again plus we were a little weary; I used my crutch which is so much easier to use than a stick, because it gives me more support. When we got to the campsite we couldn't get in as it was all shut up until 4, so we headed into town and were fortunate enough, to get a space at the end of a run, on a disabled place. It was trying to rain as we set off and by the time we reached the centre, a few hundred yards away, it was torrential. We were soaking wet, so we went into a restaurant as soon as possible, it was a great place; I had lasagne and dad had steak tartare, which is basically raw mince-meat and raw egg!!

On the way back, we called at a SPAR for some goodies, because we'd decided as the weather was set to continue, we weren't going back in for the last post. Mum and dad had been to Yres before and they had been very impressed by the ceremony, they have a 'last post' ceremony every day, they said that it had been very emotional. It was one of the main reasons that we had chosen to go to Ypres, but the rain was torrential and mum said that we would have to go half an hour early and none of us were really up to standing for that length of time, especially in the rain, it was disappointing but it couldn't be helped.

The following day we were up early and we made our way to the TYNE COT CEMETERY, it was a very impressive site; thousands of graves, monuments and names, we spent an hour looking around, it was a very moving place. We always look for names which we might have a connection to like; Fitzgerald, Lomax or Walker. Then we made our way to the port and booked in, we made a lunch of corned beef butties ready for the journey. I managed to have a nap on board again, I'd had one most days while I'd been away. We were delayed coming into port as the sea was too rough, so we had to be guided in. We were calling to see some old friends on our way back, so we headed to Cosgrove camping Milton Keynes, it took a while on the busy English roads so we didn't arrive until about 7pm. Our friends, Sheila and Rachel came soon after and we had a good three-hour catch up, it was brilliant. We had met them at a Butlins holiday, before my sister Tessa had even been born, there had been five in their family too; Jim (Sheila's husband) Rachel was my age, Lee was Kim's age and Lisa was the oldest. We had kept in touch ever since which is something like 46 years, taking turns to visit each other over the years, but it is rare now that we are all together at once.

We travelled back the rest of the way on Tuesday the 15th, Jack met me at the Van storage place, so that I could unload all my stuff. When I got home and opened all of my mail, I had received a letter off Mr Sinha, a copy of which he had sent to the DVLA but when I rang the DVLA, they said they were sending out more medical forms for me to fill in, it was ridiculous. It was so frustrating not being able to drive and be denied some independence, especially when there was no reason for me not to drive. Tes brought a Lasagne for tea which was ace, because I didn't have to cook or moan at the kids to cook either. I sorted my washing and got it outside drying out before having a nap. I'd had a brilliant time away

with my mum and dad and I didn't want the call from the
DVLA ruining my holiday high.

Chapter 15

Holidays and high days

Once I got back I spent the next day catching up on TV programmes which I'd missed while I was away and planning and sorting more trips away! I was on a roll, I paid the cruise deposit, sorted a campsite for when we went to Southport for the air show and I looked at more options for when we went touring with the van. I also filled in yet more bloody forms for the DVLA, honestly why did no one look at it with some common sense and see that all this was pointless?! It was a BOOK CLUB night and we got through lots of productive stuff, we had a trip to Mottram hall planned, so we decided on our treatments and details; we discussed our book and a new one was chosen plus we just had time for a quick catch up too.

The next day I was still in my pjs at 12; trying to muster up some energy, I could have done with a purely pj day but I had a doctor's appointment, I had to pick up the van, I needed a shower, I needed to get Tes insured for the van, I needed to phone the treatment orders through to Mottram hall and I had to call the garage for Ella plus, sort tea!! That's the trouble with being home, I always had things to do and I don't even have a job! I needed to sort myself back into a routine or I'd never get anything sorted out. At the doctors, I got my blood results my eGFR was 62, still not great BUT not the 51 it had been on my last test, to be honest I was expecting lower. So good news plus the doctors signed me off until 15th of

December. I got all my medication ordered, other than my nose rinse stuff, the doctor couldn't find it so he asked me to ask at the pharmacy; I did and they said that it would be £32 a box which would last me at the most 2 months. I was going to have to ask the ENT consultant if he could do anything, I wasn't paying that much, he came back and said I was to do a mix of salt and baking soda myself, but it is not the same at all!!

On the Friday, I had an early appoint at the Royal in Liverpool for a scan on my kidneys, afterwards me and Tes were going on to the Southport air show. I had my scan done by two different people, as one was training; it got messy with the gooey stuff they use; the nurse said she'd not seen any blockages but I heard them talking and saying that the left kidney was smaller, so we'll see when I have my appointment with Dr Shultz. Once I was done, we got in the van and we made our way to the campsite, we hooked up the van and caught the bus into town. We had a nice lunch at Frankie's and Benny's and then we went to watch the film, LEGEND with Tom Hardy, it was very good but very graphic too. Once we got back to the van, we had a lovely couple of brews before the kids descended, they had driven up after work so that they could come and see the airshow with us, but they were late because they'd gone wrong and they said the site looked dodgy!

The following morning, we were all up and dressed and all sorted by 8.30, off we trekked but as soon as we got into Southport we hit traffic, we tried a different route and found the disabled area luckily. Lots of people were already there, and it was only 9.45, I had my wheelchair because we weren't sure how far we'd have to go, we managed to find a space on the beach wall and set up camp. We had a really good day – the weather was great, the airshow was outstanding and so entertaining, I loved the red arrows and the Vulcan, plus we had such a laugh too. When I needed the toilet, Tes escorted me because I'd come in my wheelchair, I didn't have my crutch with me and as there was a massive queue, I used the disabled one as I couldn't stand that long but I was met with more than one judging look! Not everyone who is 'disabled' in some way, looks like it. When it was all finished we waited a good while to let the worst of the traffic disperse, then we set off in search of somewhere to eat, but everywhere was understandably busy, we ended up taking a shortcut through a housing estate and finding a pub. We had a lovely meal and then we returned to the van, where we saw the effects of the sun on us all, I had the reddest face!

Next day I wasn't awake until 10.15am, but I was still not ready to get up, every time I moved it hurt, I ached all over. Tes was stressing trying to rally Jack because she wanted him to take her to town, I don't think that he wanted to but bless him he got ready and they went about 11. Then peace descended. I had another brew and then made cheese toasties for me and Ella, then I slowly got myself sorted. I went for a shower but I couldn't figure out where the lights were, so I spent a good 5 to 10 mins cleaning the floor and prepping with the light off, waving at the sensor and accepting that I may have to have a shower in the dark. Then just as I was about to shut the door I heard a roar and was treated to another fly past by the red arrows, fantastic! Then as I locked the door and walked in, the lights came on, thank goodness, I had a quick shower but then I realised that I'd forgotten my clean clothes.

Following all the excitement, there followed several chill days, it was getting harder to get up each morning and keeping motivated was becoming tougher too; probably because I'd had so many holidays and I was so out of routine, plus I was knackered because I was doing more. Part of me wanted to make sure that I had things planned in, so that I wasn't wasting my time and life away; then another part of me just wanted to do nothing all of the time. I'm sure a healthy mix of the two was the answer but I still didn't seem to be getting it right; was I doing too much at once, was not allowing myself enough rest days or did I just try and keep up with everyone else? It was probably a mixture of all three, but at least I WAS getting out and doing things, so I was on the right track at least.

Wednesday 23rd September - MY 47TH BIRTHDAY!

I felt every bit my age, I coloured my hair, covering up my increasingly grey roots. I met Tes, Kim and mum in Nantwich and we went to a lovely little café called Ginger and Pickles, I had a huge afternoon tea, which was very nice but I only managed half of it, so I had a goody bag to take home. It had been a long, long time since the four of us had been out together, just us, we should have gotten a pic! Once I got back home I went for a nap and I had a good two hours, I felt rough but rallied, I had an extra hydrocortisone to help me through the night, we were going to see James Bay at Manchester Opera house. Unfortunately, Ella didn't manage to get an early finish from work and arrived home at 6.10, she had a quick change and we somehow managed to get the 6.34 train to Manchester.

We arrived at Manchester Piccadilly and Jack had arranged with Tim (who was having the 4th ticket) to meet him opposite the taxi rank, so Tim could pick us up. We asked Jack if he was sure where we were meeting and he assured us that he did, so we walked to where he thought and waited for a good 25 mins. Jack couldn't contact Tim because his phone had died. At this point as we were getting concerned that we would miss the show, Jack got a call from Tim; he had been the other side of the station but he had to go back to his flat so that he could contact Jack. So we walked back to the station and out the other side, where there were more taxis and we waited for him to pick us up, piss up in a brewery comes to mind!!

When we finally got to the venue, we had our bags checked and I always have a bottle of water with me, especially in the evenin. The security man said,

"You can't take the water in."

"Oh, please I have condition where I drink a lot."

"No sorry, rules is rules."

"But I have a brain tumour!"

He then quickly ushered us in.

"Omg mum I can't believe you just did that!"

"Oh, I don't use it often"

We got to our seats just as the second support artist was finishing but in plenty of time for James Bay. Probably because I'd already been out, my body was tired and so I was very jerky, people probably thought that I was just sit-down dancing! Luckily, we were in the circle and everyone sat down, it was a fantastic gig, we all loved it. It finished at 22.40, Tim drove us back to the station, however, we were way too late to get the 22.36 train so we had to get the 23.38. The kids went off to get food, and they ended up at 'Subway' outside of the station, because they'd only had a snack on the train going, I just had water. At the time, I didn't know where they were, so I was stressing once the train pulled into the station. (my clock said 23.33) I thought they were hiding and watching me stress out but they were waiting for their foot longs! On the train, they ate their food then Jack abandoned us for friends on the train, me and Els were knackered and she was at work for 7.30 the following day, at least I could have a lie in.

I had a very chilled day the following day, the day after I was making lists of things which needed doing and setting out short and long-term goals. I was feeling that I was slowly getting sorted and getting in some sort of routine, which allowed me to get things done more efficiently; I loved being away, it was great having time out but I liked being home too because I did like routine. When I finished work in July, I'd said to myself that I was going to give myself some time for my body to properly recover and so I was trying to allow my body the time it needed, whenever I could. Before I had my operation I struggled with focussing on anything other than my operation and at this time my focus was on 2016 and all the travels that I had planned, so many of the things on my to do list were around making sure that the trips were organised.

That weekend one of Ella's best friends Katie, who had been her best friend since they were about five and had come on numerous holidays with us, was having a 21st birthday party. I called her my second daughter and her mum Claire called Ella her 3rd daughter (because Katie had a sister), so I had been invited along too, I had been stressing about what I was going to wear since the invite arrive, because it was fancy dress. Ella had ordered a 20's flapper dress, accessories and even a wig and she looked amazing. I had decided to go as the white rabbit from Alice in wonderland; I wore white trousers, a white shirt, a blue jacket and I had ears and glasses, which I had borrowed from Tor, I thought that I had some face paint, but I couldn't find any so much to Ella's amusement I used sudocrem and talc!! At the time, I thought that I had looked ok but there were many pictures and I just looked fat!! It was great though with everyone dressed up, I only stayed a couple of hours, Ella wasn't drinking so she drove me home and then went back again.

Someone had reversed into Ella while she was at a junction, so I was going to the car rental place to pick up a car with her. Jack dropped us off, because I wasn't allowed to drive and Ella obviously didn't have her car. We had been given a time to go and pick it up but when we got there it wasn't ready, so we had to wait. The young man serving us was trying his best to chat Ella up and much to her dismay I sat down and left him to it, he was asking her all sorts, even where she was off to that night!! Bless her she was a little oblivious to it all, she doesn't realise how gorgeous she is, inside and out. The following day Ella was due to give blood so I said that I would go with her, Jack was already a donor and after everything I had been through she wanted to give blood too. So, Ella and I went to Nantwich Civic hall and she signed up, they pin pricked her thumb to test for iron levels I think, but when they came to take blood things didn't go to plan. The nurse came over and strapped her arm and tapped her arm to bring up the veins but she couldn't find one to use, so she called over another nurse to have a look but unfortunately, she couldn't find one either.

"I'm sorry but we aren't allowed to try if we don't think that we will be successful."

"Oh.....right.."

"Your veins just aren't very good, I'm sorry. You can come back in 5 years."

"Five years?" Turning to me she said "That's your fault!"

She was truly gutted that she couldn't give blood she had wanted to do her bit, we were a bit shocked at the five years bit though. The next few days I struggled to do much at all, other than bits and bobs, chilling and naps. One thing which I did do; I had gone to Tessa's but she wasn't there so I thought that I would have some fun. Do you know that film called 'Sleeping with the enemy'? Well she's like that, she has to have all her tins facing a particular way, she has her cushions just so and her towels all lined up; so, I go around turning things but not so that it is really obvious, so that it takes a few days for her to realise what I've done. It really is the small things in life which can keep you most amused isn't it?

My old work friend, Tracey called for a catch up and later Joanna too. A couple of days later Tor text and asked if she could come early to book club, I said of course, I had nowhere to go, we had quite an honest conversation about where I was at physically. I said I was just so tired and feeling a little worn out by it all at present. She said I've got something I've wanted to ask you since it all began, I thought oh god what?!

"How do you not get depressed? How do you stay so positive?"

My answer was this,

"I truly believe that some people are predisposed to being negative and this adversely affects their mood and I'm not one of those people, plus I want to stay strong for the kids. I don't feel like I can afford to falter as it's a slippery slope, so I work tirelessly to keep myself busy, occupied and motivated. One of the reasons that I have had so many holidays and things to look forward to is that it takes me away from my reality and gives me something else to focus on."

I did go on to say that I still had moments of 'why me' and struggled with the fact that my tiredness seemed never ending, but I tried to not let it take over me. Tor is one of the happiest, warmest people I know but she admits that things can get on top of her sometimes, so she said she wanted to know how I did it. I think that when we are faced with huge obstacles, more often than not, we find that we rise to the challenge. Then later that day I came across the following quote,

'The body has approximately eleven organ systems all doing different things at the same time. In order to keep us functioning or well, alive, they need one voice. A leader. A master. And, in our brains, that job belongs to the pituitary gland. It senses the body's needs before they even arise, working non-stop. The Pituitary gland communicates with all the other glands, telling them when to produce the vital hormones we need to function. It keeps everything running smoothly, in perfect order. There's no denying it, it has the toughest job in the place." From Grey's anatomy.

I sort of already knew it but seeing it in black and white had more of an impact, my hypothalamus is damaged too, so that just adds to the problems. Later on, I watched this programme about retraining your brain - it was aimed at athletes and getting more out of your body and mind over matter. There were lots of interesting bits which seemed even more poignant after my talk with Tor earlier in the day, I found it very interesting and I do believe that our bodies are helped or hindered by our minds.

Sunday 4th October, Mum and dad were leaving to go back to Spain the following day, so myself, Jack and Ella went to Tessa's about 1.30, as always everyone (immediate family) had gathered to say their farewells. It's just so great when everyone gets together, but nine people all competing to speak and talking is a bit draining. I'm sure that most families are the same but it left me with a banging headache!! Tes brought me home at 4pm I had a buttie, then I changed into my pj's again and came upstairs where it's dark and quiet. I got up at 7.15 but I still had headache so I took some morphine and went back to bed. I was in pain so much of the time with one thing or another; it was probably a contributing factor in why I was so tired as well.

I was going out for lunch the next day with Ella, mum and dad, so I needed to get up and have a shower, it left me feeling sickie so I took a cyclizine tablet, it didn't help massively and then I felt dizzy too, I was feeling properly out of sorts for some reason. We had a lovely meal at the Dysart arms in Bunbury. Ella wanted it to be her treat, so I had to warn mum and dad not to moan about the prices of everything and not to say 'it's so much cheaper in Spain, which they have a tendency to do! Afterwards, we drove through the village to look at the buildings, which had been used in a recent TV series, 'Home fires'. It was clear which houses had or were being used, because they're making a second series, as they had the crosses in the windows to protect from bombs!! There were big hugs all round, saying goodbye, it's always emotional; they go for 6 months and normally I will go and see them at some point, but it's still a long time.

While I was spending some time 'doing nothing' I thought that I would try and do those jobs which you just don't seem to get around to, so I sorted out videos and pictures, then I backed them up plus I cleared some space on my computer too, I was very pleased with myself, so a good day all in all! After tea Ella wanted to try on some things for the cruise so she did some modelling of her clothes, she put one dress on, which had been Tessa's, it was very glamorous;

but she had a devil's own job getting it on, it kept getting stuck and rucking up.

"Mum stop laughing, help me!"

I nearly cried laughing, it's always the small things!! We went through all of her clothes and she had got some lovely stuff to take with her on the cruise, it's a great occasion to really go to town.

One of my old dancing friends, Ali came around, she's been through a lot bless her and we talked about coping or appearing to cope but that we may not process as we should. I hoped that I didn't get through all the physical stuff then suffer mentally after!? How do you know? Maybe one day it will hit me and I will be floored, all that I knew was that at that time, I had to just keep going. I woke up the next day feeling very ropey so I went down for drinks, because in the morning I am always really thirsty, then I retreated back to bed to see if I could shake my headache. After a couple of hours, I was still feeling much the same so I thought do I just give in and stay in bed or do I power on through? In the end, I cracked on and sorted out my spare room, I have always found that occupying your mind can be a very good tactic.

On Friday the 9th, I had another appointment at the Royal in Liverpool, I was seeing Dr Alexander in nephrology but he was running an hour or more, late. I had the pleasure of being weighed again 89.3kg. Oh joy, it was what I thought, it seemed to have stabilised; my height was 5'5", I had always thought I was 5'6" so now I seemed even fatter! I was in with the doctor for 1.5 hours, I didn't see the main man but the lady I saw was lovely, she was very thorough, she asked me lots of questions and examined me. Then when she took it to her boss he said that it wasn't kidney disease from the results that he had, despite the low EGFR result,

'GFR - glomerular filtration rate is the best test to measure your level of kidney function and determine your stage of kidney disease. Your doctor can calculate it from the results of your blood creatinine test, your age, body size and gender. A GFR below 60 for three months or more or a GFR above 60 with kidney damage (marked by high levels of albumin in your urine) indicates chronic kidney disease. Your doctor will want to investigate the cause of your kidney disease and continue to check your kidney function to help plan your treatment.'

Mine had been as low as 51 and had been coming down gradually since my operation, so to hear it wasn't kidney disease was good because it had been a real concern but on the other hand, no new miracle meds to sort out whatever the issue was. He recommended a rheumatologist, to see if he could help with the possibility that it was an autoimmune problem. He did add, that if he had my 24-hour urine results, and they contained protein, then he would need to conduct more tests. The results seemed to have gone astray, it was only months later that they surfaced and they did show that there was in fact protein in my samples. We love Ikea so we called on our way back and had a lovely lunch of meatballs and chips, then cheesecake; no miracle drugs but no dire news either, so a good day in my book.

The day after, my 'hospital bestie' Sheila was coming to visit, so Ella picked her up from the station and took us to Nantwich. We had a brief look at the market and then made our way to Ginger and Pickles, a cute little cafe and we just had hot drinks, so that we could talk without distraction, so much to catch up on and we did have a lot in common. We had a bit more of a look around before going onto lunch at Harrison's, we had the most amazing tomato and roasted pepper soup and sandwiches. We talked about our attitudes, the changes in our lives' trajectory and how we are lucky that we have choices in our lives; some people get what we're going through and others struggle. Having someone who had been through similar issues, understood my fears, problems and choices; we talk openly about how we felt about our futures in honest, open conversation. Ella picked us up again about 3pm bless her and we carried on yakking until 5.45 when Jack took us to the station to drop Sheila off again.

The following day as expected my feet and legs were really hurting, I felt like I was recovering from a marathon not a brief walk and day of talking. After my discussion with Sheila, I researched and ordered a magnetic bracelet and other bits to see if they would help with my pain, I really didn't want to get hooked on pain medication and take it regularly, so that my body would need more and more to address the pain. Another thing that I was going to do was to try my best to research and apply more healthy eating and routines which would improve my situation. The doctors could only do so much and I was frankly fed up of waiting around, plus I didn't want to just keep taking the drugs, I wanted to do as much as I could to help myself, so that means understanding what's going on with my body and addressing the issues.

Yet another project, I was itching to get started on was my book but I was conscious of setting up my business so that I could begin to generate some money first. I did some figures and as long as I don't go mad I should be alright with the money I had, I had some benefits which helped with my household costs, I also had my bond money to cover travelling for a few years. Anything I get extra would cover the gap in my household bills firstly and then depending on how much I earned, it would prolong the travelling and help me have better quality choices. I would need to manage my money well and work towards being able to set up and run an online business which I could do even if I wasn't feeling great, so if everything went to plan I should be ok.......then again when does anything I do ever do go to plan?

Chapter 16

Spa Spa

On Friday the 16th of October, I was off to Mottram Hall, part of the QHotel group, for a spa weekend with the book club girls. Elaine and I were going for two nights the other three were coming up on the Saturday morning and staying the second night with us. Elaine picked me up about 12 and we stopped off, for an early lunch at Sandbach, a lovely historic town, then we were off again; unfortunately, the GPS let us down a bit. GPS is brilliant, amazing, spectacular when it is working and taking you the right way, however, when it is having a weird off day, it is pants!! I have been taken up 2m wide streets in my motorhome, taken to the back entrance of hotels and just taken to the middle of nowhere, but I continue to put my faith in them, we managed to find the right entrance to Mottram Hall, eventually. It is an imposing, magnificent building with beautiful grounds, it's the type of place where I always want to put on my posh telephone voice.

We checked in and dropped our bags in our lovely room and went for our treatment; we had both chosen to have a massage and it was so relaxing. I do love a massage, if I had enough money I would have a massage every week, it I had lots and lots of money I would employ a masseuse full time. After our treatments, we went to the spa area; there is a lovely pool and jacuzzi with seating areas around, there is an amazing outside area with a hot tub, sauna and steam room too. We spent a while just chilling, unwinding and chatting away; I have known Elaine since I was 4 years old and so she knows everything that I have been through and I do her, so we understand each other very well. I think Elaine and I are most alike; we both tend to look at things and weigh things up, we are both pretty laid back and calm and we both view the world in a very similar way. As a result, spending time with each other is always a pleasure especially in such glorious surroundings. In the evening, we had a wonderful three course meal in the restaurant but we were back in our room for 9pm; we watched Warrick Davies in an interview, it was fascinating and a great end to the day.

The following day, we were up by 9am and down to breakfast, I rarely eat breakfast so I wasn't that hungry, I just had a little fruit and half a choc croissant. Then we went back to the room to wait for the girls, they arrived about 10.40, we actually heard them before we saw them, because they had parked outside of our room. They came to our room and there were brews all round and a good catch up, subjects covered were; children, morals, choices and insecurities, it doesn't matter what we talk about, we all have very similar views. Before we knew it was 1.30 and we needed to go for our lunch, I got half way there and had to come back because I needed to get some medication, as for some reason I suddenly felt really sick. Our lunch was an afternoon tea, which as you know, is my favourite but when we went to check in they didn't have us booked in. Despite not having us listed they just sat us down no problem, it was lovely as usual, we couldn't eat it all but as we were eating later it was pointless bringing away goody bags.

While the others went to the spa area again, I stayed for a nap, I felt really dizzy and I continued to, whilst I was going off to sleep; I was woken after about an hour by noise in the next room then I needed a wee! I took an extra hydrocortisone to give me a boost, the girls got back about 6.30 and we all got ready to go to the restaurant for our meal. As the night before, the food was lovely and the five of us had such a laugh as always, after the meal we then moved onto to the cocktail bar. There was alcohol flowing but I only had one glass, I stayed up until 10.45pm!! We covered more subjects like; holidays as kids and abroad as youngsters away from parents, we talked about me writing a book; everyone thought that I should write a book about my experiences. This is a quote from my diary which perfectly illustrates my forgetful brain,

'I said something funny tonight, but I've already forgotten what!!'

The day after, we met to go down for breakfast about 9am but there was a huge queue and we weren't sure whether we'd have enough time to eat before our treatments. One of the managers came and explained that everyone had come down at once but they were working hard to minimise the wait; we were asked to wait in the bar once our names had been taken, and we started with brews, after only 10 minutes we were called for breakfast. We managed to have a relaxed breakfast before it was time for our treatments. I had a lovely foot and leg massage and a toe polish which was heavenly. Elaine left after her treatment and the rest of us chilled by the pool and in the outdoor jacuzzi. Then Tor and Debs went off to have their treatments and Joanna and I had brews and a catch up, talk often centres around work, because it's easier to talk to someone in your profession because they understand the stresses easier.

Once the girls had finished their treatments we met up for more brews once and chatter, like most groups of good friends we literally never stop; it's like a relay team someone has always got the baton. We had had the most amazing weekend, it was just so chilled and relaxing, we all get on so well and trust each other, it just gets better and better. Personally, I think that having great friends is priceless, you can't buy better therapy; I felt so fortunate to have them all, plus I had other fantastic friends too. I think as you get older your time is more precious, so you choose to spend it with people who you love and trust; those people who don't add to your life or negatively impact upon it, you choose to spend less and less time with until they are no longer part of your life and you are left with the cream of the crop.

I got home late afternoon and I thought that Ella was going out for tea with a lad who'd been pursuing her for weeks but he then he let her down at the last minute, I just thought more fool him, Ella is a catch and she was strong and I knew that she wouldn't give him the time of day after that. So as a consolation, we ordered a takeaway, I'd not eaten since breakfast, but I think that I was still full after a weekend of stuffing myself. So, we sat eating pizza and putting the world to rights, Ella is very determined and strong when she wants to be but she doesn't like confrontation, if it had of been me I think that I may have given the lad a piece of my mind. Jack put his two penneth worth in too, by saying I told you so!

Probably not the best time but his comments, on the said boy, were probably spot on.

The next day was Tessa's birthday, and she had managed to get two complimentary tickets for a local gym and spa, Alvaston Hall, it is part of the Western hotel group. So, we spent a lovely couple of hours chilling in the spa, Tessa ventured into the pool but I was happy to chill on my bed, it wasn't like I'd been doing much chilling lately! We did a bit of people watching as you do, we did discuss what people might say about us, scary thought; in the past people have guessed we were sisters, some people have even got us mixed up. On one occasion in a club, where we had gone to look at a band, a lady thought that we were 'together', after when Tes continued whispering in my ear, I told her to back off, it did make us laugh.

I had decided when I left work before the Summer that I would take a few months off to recoup as it were but I had begun to feel restless in between my trips, so I had to started to think more about setting up a business online. It seemed the perfect option for me, as it wasn't physical and it could easily be fitted into my life, I had lots of material to use for my website but I had a lot of work, yet to do to make it ready to be put onto a website. One of the first things which I need to decide upon was a name, I liked something like; Anna Gray group improvement programmes but then someone said don't put your name to it, then someone else was saying what is the acronym for it? I was beginning to realise that even the name needed some serious thought, especially because it would be the basis of all the marketing and promotions.

To feel more organised and business like, I had set up a mini office in my dining area, I have a kitchen diner with a breakfast bar where we eat and a folding table which extends when we have more people round. I sorted a cabinet which would house all the documents which I needed and the table next to it would serve as my desk. I had a high-backed chair or an office chair which I could use, so that I wouldn't get too achy. So, I was all set up to start doing some more focussed work, I had done a lot of my degree sat there so I knew that I could work well there. The other thing about being in the kitchen diner was that it was the warmest room in the house, so in October it was the perfect, cosy place, plus the kettle was handy for brews. So I was all set up and ready to go.....

I was still trying to watch what I ate and to look for non-medicinal options to help with my pain and fatigue; I felt better for doing as much as I could to help myself and reflexology and massages were both part of my plan. My former colleague Trina was doing both and I felt more at ease with having her do my treatments, she was still training but she was a skilled clinician and I always felt better after any treatment. While I still wasn't able to drive Jack would often drop me for my appointments and Trina would drop me back off, I couldn't have ask for a better service. She is now fully trained and she runs her own business 'Trina Bailey therapies'. We would normally have a bit of a catch up because both our lives had changed so much since we had first met, then she would do my treatment, which I loved and I would try and go home and rest up for the rest of the day to get the full benefit from my treatment. I received my 'energy' bracelet, worth a try and some circulation socks, to see if they helped at night time; I already had my bracelet for circulation and pain, my dad swore by his magnetic supports and he doesn't do any sort of doctors and resists taking medication for as long as he can.

MI also had a new symptom, pain in my knees, they had begun hurting, so on top of the pain and issues with my feet walking, coming down stairs was now causing me some degree of difficulty and pain. At night time, my pain seemed to be particularly acute, whether it was due to the day's actions or just the fact that my mind wasn't occupied with other things, I didn't know but it was becoming more and more of an issue. Trying to get off to sleep wasn't normally an issue but I was often woken with restless legs (your legs just seemed to have a mind of their own and want to move and they just won't stay still) and such bad pains in my legs too. My legs are normally burning up, so it does help if my legs are out of the covers to keep them cooler, however, most times I have to take some medication to ease my legs. It was a nightly challenge which I dreaded, because I was getting such a poor night's sleep most nights, it meant that I was having naps in the afternoons on a regular basis.

My hair had begun to grow back, after having lost my hair in patches after my radiation, but it looked very odd and tufty, so I was still covering it up with my fringe across it. The other issue that I had with tuft regrowth, was that it had a kink in it, I have always had poker straight hair. In the 80s and 90s I would have it permed but the year before I got all my symptoms, my hair started going curly. It was bizarre and I couldn't figure out why, I thought I was going through the change and my hormones were affecting it; I was right about the hormones affecting it but it wasn't menopause it was the tumour. was having my hair cut by Tessa and it was even more of a big deal for me than it had been before, she claims that I am her worst client because I am so picky and fussy. So, I was keeping my fingers crossed that I would like it and that it didn't make me look even fatter! Tes was also trying to straighten my tuft so that it didn't stick out everywhere. When Tes had finished I looked in the mirror, I didn't hate it but didn't love it either, I would need to wash it and make an effort to style it which I wasn't great at. That's another thing which I would have, if I had the money, someone to do my hair whenever I needed it, with having a sister as a hairdresser I rarely paid for anything, but it's not quite the same as having your own personal hairdresser is it?

I love a good true story and I watched UNBROKEN; it's a brilliant film, a true story about an American athlete, who went on to be a soldier in WW2 and was taken prisoner by the Japanese, he was then persecuted by one of the guards. I really enjoyed it, it was another reminder of the power of the mind to withstand and help your body to fight harder, in times of need. I am a true believer in the power of the mind, athletes use it, powerful business people use it and those working with children, too. Not long after I had started working as a learning mentor, I was working with a bright young man who was constantly making poor choices, he was one of those people who could use his leadership skills for good or bad and I was trying to point him in the right direction. He was saying that it was hard making the right choices and being good and I was saying that if he put his mind to it he could do anything. At that point, he picked up a piece of paper, he had been scribbling on, scrunched it up and threw it at the bin, but it hit one wall and then another before going in the bin, it was a one off.

"I'll bet you can't do that again." "Tell yourself that you can't do it........over and over....keep saying it. Now throw the paper."

He looked at me a little bemused but he was used to my weirdness and he threw it and he missed,

"Now tell yourself that you are going to do what you did before, you're going to hit one wall and then it will hit the other and then it will go in. Convince yourself that you will do it, leave no doubt in your mind."

So, he threw the paper and it did just as I had described and it went in. You should have seen his face, he was blown away.

"You see? That's the power of positive thinking!"

This kid was one of my toughest challenges, he was an angry young man and each time I saw him across the yard I would wave madly and if he didn't wave back I would chase him until he did. Years later I saw him at a local carnival, I was there to watch a show, he was leading a large group of young men all looking a little menacing, so he'd obviously taken the wrong path, but when he saw me he waved, I had to laugh to myself, this big tough kid must have been frightened that I would chase him again. I waved back and just smiled, I just wish that I had had more of an affect on his other behaviours.

A few days later, I needed to pick up a prescription from the doctors but Ella had so much on she was struggling to fit me in, the frustrations of not being able to drive! When I went to collect my prescription, the girl (whom I knew, she was a pupil from school) she asked me if it was CD, I was like WHAT!? It turns out that it meant controlled drug, in my arsenal of drugs I had several 'controlled drugs' which you have to collect from the doctors themselves and sign for, so that they know who has them. They were my patches; I was reducing them so at this point, I was just wearing a half patch. It says clearly on the instructions do not cut, but what was going to happen? Turns out nothing at all.

Jack's girlfriend, Terri had been away all Summer with her mum and family in America, her mum Bernie, had been receiving treatment there. When she came back Bernie seemed to be doing well and everyone was so happy for her. Unfortunately, Jack and Terri decided that they would split up, then one-night a couple of weeks later, Jack came in and said that Terri had text, saying that her mum had only weeks to live. It was such a shock, only weeks after thinking that things were going well, it was awful and Jack felt that he was in a difficult position; he wanted to be there for Terri but he wasn't with her anymore. Bernie had been through so much and it all seemed to be going well, we didn't know what had happened but it was devastating. It was just awful, I felt so upset for everyone, she was such a lovely lady and mum, plus she had a big family and circle of friends; what can you say to someone when they get that news? It was just so very, very sad.

Later that night I was up in pain and Jack saw my light on and popped his head round the door. He was really struggling with the news, he said,

"I just don't understand mum why?! Just as things are getting on track, these things happen. I've had the toughest two weeks with Terri and everything, then her mum, it's just not fair. And you, you've got all these things I don't understand, it's just not fair. "

What can you say? Life can be horribly unfair but sometimes it's unfair in your favour, this time it just wasn't. It's horrible to see those we love suffer so much and as a family we've been pretty lucky up until recently, Jack and Ella still had all of their grandparents. I had no words to help him in that moment, I could only be there for him. Ella was really sad too and said she that she just wanted to cry all the time, I think that it was just too close to home. She'd been painting her room because it needed it and she said it had really helped to calm her down. Jacks was just being very quiet.

A few days later we had heard that Bernie had been moved to St Luke's hospice, which is a marvellous, calming place by all accounts. I was sorting tea, getting some food prepped, Jack had asked me to do some food to take with us, because we had arranged to go and visit Bernie. Then Jack came down and he said that we couldn't go now because Bernie had taken a turn for the worst and only family could visit. The kids were so upset, maybe it's because it's really the only person, other than Jane my friend who took her own life, that they've really known who was that poorly. I had had a conversation with Tes, about people close dying and she said,

" Yeah, well if it had of been you!!"

"I'd meant mum and dad or their other grandparents."

But it just showed again how people had been thinking, I knew that I had been ill and a worry for people but it was different for me. I had to keep strong, I knew it was the best thing for me but the kids' reaction had shown me that maybe behind closed doors away from me they had cried tears for me too. In the days to come, we all struggled with the news, how her immediate family and friends must have felt was beyond words. Both Jack and Ella were visibly upset, they each had their own ways to deal with it; as ever Jack tended to be quiet, Ella wanted to talk. I was glad we were all away the following week in the van, but in some ways, it would be another reminder to them how limited I was, because most of the time they don't see it really. I wasn't the mum I had been only a few years earlier, to me at that time, the former me seemed to be 'Superwoman'!

Chapter 17

The three Musketeers, on tour

We had decided that we would all go away in the van, the last week of October, I was a little apprehensive for all three of us to be in such a confined space for a week but we'd just have to get on with it. I'd chosen a site in Abersoch, Wales, it was somewhere that I'd never been but I'd heard good reports about it plus, it was only about two hours away and the site itself wasn't far from the town. Yet again, we had trouble with the van, so we had to get it jumped again but luckily it started; when we got home, we loaded up quickly keeping the van running. We finally set off about 2.45pm, we had a few hours journey in front of us, but I just wanted to get there, get organised and chill. Jack was in the front because apparently, I wasn't a good passenger, I'd only travelled a couple of miles with Ella driving and me in the front too. It was Ella's first time driving the van but it didn't seem to faze her at all, Jack couldn't drive because he wasn't on the insurance and I didn't have a license!

We travelled so far before stopping off at the services, on the A55, to get fuel and food; we were a little nervous about the van starting again but it restarted no problem, which was a relief and the Subways, despite being on flat bread, were actually really good. Ella was doing so well driving, she wasn't nervous at all and the van was doing well on the flat but it laboured up hills somewhat. It would be nearly 6 by the time we got there, but I'd left a message with the site, that we would be arriving a bit late, so I was hoping that we would still be allowed in. The first chunk of the journey was on fast roads but the latter half to the site, was along windy Welsh roads in the dark; the final mile or so, as guided by the trusty GPS was long and very narrow about a mile from town, it was that narrow that at times we were catching the hedges with the wing mirrors, which stick out from the van.

When we finally got there about 6 pm, we all heaved a big sigh of relief but this was short lived when we realised that the reception was closed. By chance there was a man walking up to the house, behind the reception.

"We're closed!"

I explained that I had booked and that I had telephoned ahead to explain that we'd been delayed, he checked their records and there was nothing. I was thinking; is this the right site, did I book it, didn't I get a confirmation? It was then that I realised I had conversed about the booking over email, so then he checked the emails and luckily found an email confirming our booking. As it was really dark, with few lights, on the site, he told us to park by the toilet block on the grass, he said that we may want to move in the morning, on to a hardstanding pitch because there was a lot of rain forecasted.

The van was a mess so we got about getting sorted, by the time we were done, it was nearly 8.30 so I just cooked the kids some pasta, I wasn't fussed. We had a good signal, so we watched the X factor after figuring out that the mobiles were affecting the signal, so we had to keep them away from the TV. At 9.30pm I was ready for bed but I couldn't find my earplugs, I hadn't slept without them for about 3 years; I began wearing them when I was first ill and going to bed early, when there was still noise in the house, now I was just used to having them in, I knew that I would struggle without them. I was wrong, I got off straight away, despite the kids having the TV on, then I woke about 11.30 in pain so I took one tramadol and some morphine. In the end, not a bad night's sleep, I woke a few times because of the noise of the wind and seagulls, so I'd still look for some ear plugs!

We woke about 9am eager to see what it was like in the daylight, we had a great view of the sea from where we were, high above it. I felt a bit rough after the previous day but I took my medication and I felt better after a drink of orange juice and cup of tea. I'd not been able to pay the night before but when I went to check in after my brew the reception was still closed. We moved the van but the hard standings didn't have quite the view we'd had but we thought that it was better than getting stuck in the mud; we then tried unsuccessfully to put up the awning which had come with the van, so we packed it back up again.

It took another age to get the bikes down from the rack and to sort them out, we finally set off to Abersoch, about 12.30. I'd not ridden a bike, in forever but it was less than a mile to town, so I thought that I would be ok; you know how they say you never forget how to ride a bike? Apparently, I could, not only was I struggling energy wise, I was also struggling with my balance too, so it was flippin hard work; Jack kept stopping to check on me, Ella was having her own battle, but we all made it eventually. We had a brief look around before Jack exclaimed that he was starving, never just hungry but starving, so we went into 'Vaynol', we sat overlooking the water and we had a tasty lunch, it was lovely and chilled. Next, we got on our bikes and rode a short distance to explore the beach area and sailing club, the kids went onto the beach while I sat on some seats from a bar which wasn't open, watching. It reminded me of when they were young and they loved to explore rock pools and mess about on the beach, they were no different, they still liked to, it made me smile to myself.

Then the weather began to look decidedly dodgy, so we set off back to the van, on the way back it was even harder work because it was slightly up hill; you rarely notice when you are going down, I was very out of breath, then my bloody pedal fell off, luckily it was just around the corner from the site. We got back to the van about 3.15 to a chilli, coming along nicely in the slow cooker, it had kept the van very warm which was perfect. We also managed to get the WIFI code, so we spent a good half hour or so playing before putting on Jurassic World. We all love the Jurassic series, Jack watched it when he was about 3 years old and he wasn't frightened by it, he had bedding and he had every dinosaur toy going. When we had gone to America, with my mum and dad, when Jack was 9 years old, me and the kids had gone to Universal and Jack had loved it. He had his own money and he went off to buy one of the Jurassic dinosaurs; he came back and said,

"When I paid the lady said with tax that is 10 dollars.... I told her that I didn't want to pay tax!"

Bless him, I still don't think that he wants to pay tax. We really enjoyed just chilling watching it, then we ate the chilli which was nice; it had been a gamble because I hadn't had any chilli powder, which I normally put in, so I had put in some of Jack's hot sauce instead. It had been a great first day, but for me full on, so I had another early night and luckily while we had been in town I had managed to get some ear plugs to use.

I was up by 9.20am, a brew the first order of the day, then I had a lovely shower in the toilet block; they aren't always so nice, so it was a pleasant surprise. When the kids were younger we had a folding camper and I tended to go on Caravan Club sites because they were always good sites; they had play areas for the kids, big pitches, great toilet blocks and they didn't allow rowdy groups on! Jack and Ella wanted to go into town again but after yesterday I was more than happy to stay at the van, however Jack wanted to bike into town whereas Ella wanted to walk. They couldn't agree and after a llloooonnnnggggg 'discussion' Jack rode and Ella walked!

Anyway they went off and I did a little tidying and sorting then all of a sudden, the electrics went off, I checked everything twice and I couldn't sort it, as it was the end of the season there was only a few caravans and it looked like some of them weren't occupied, so I couldn't see anyone to check if it was just ours or everyone's. So, I went up to reception as I'd still not managed to book in, I had a proper laugh with them over the electrics but I still couldn't book in as they don't take cards and I didn't have enough cash. The electrics were a more general issue, not me tripping something thank god, so they sorted whatever the problem was and it was back on again. The kids weren't gone long at all, they were back about 12.30 just before some really heavy rain came down. We then spent the majority of the afternoon watching the Sons of anarchy which we had become a little addicted to, someone had recommended it to me. On paper, it doesn't sound like something I might watch; a group of mainly ugly, fierce biker blokes and how they get themselves into all sorts of trouble, but I loved it!

I had another good sleep so after dozing off after taking my medication at 9am, I didn't get up until 10.15am, the kids were awake but playing on their phones until I woke, bless them. We had decided that we would go into Pwllheli and have a look around, it was too far to bike so we were going in the van, it's a bit of a faff because you have to unplug and make safe but there's not that much to do in Abersoch and the kids had been twice. That's the only draw-back with a motorhome you can't explore the same, you normally have to rely on public transport. The entrance to the site was quite steep and we got stuck going up, so Ella had to reverse it and take a good run up; so she had another go and this time she managed it. When we arrived in Pwllheli and we were trying to find somewhere to park up, Jack who was in the back, was desperate for the toilet and a number two at that!! I'd cleaned the toilet, so I was reluctant to let him,

"Oh, Jack can't you wait we won't be long?"

"I can't mum, if I don't go, I will have quite an accident!" (his language was far more coarse!)

Whilst that was going on, Ella had found a space at the end of a run, Ella did really well parking up, because it is wide

220

it took several attempts to get it tucked in. We locked up and had a look about, we bought some bits and bobs; I wanted to get some meat but when I went up to a man with a van on the market, he could only sell me 10 steaks not 3, so I decided against it. We really wanted to eat fish and chips but the queue at the only place we could find was huge and the kids lost patience, I'd had to get my folding stick out, my legs were not playing ball; I thought that I'd escaped the effects of the bike ride but obviously not. We sadly ended up in Subway which was pretty poor, don't get me wrong I love a subway but I had hoped for better.

When we got in the van and headed back to Abersoch, I saw a sign for another beach and a parking sign, so we followed it and parked up; we weren't sure though, how we'd get back to the main road as there was a tricky hill. I sat on a veranda belonging to a closed cafe on a deckchair which Jack had carried down for me, whilst the kids went for a wander again. They only had trainers on, so there was a good chance that they would get messy; there was quite a few people about walking and with dogs, I could imagine it being glorious there in the Summer months. They came back after a while and they weren't too bad, we got back in the van and luckily made it up the hill, no issue at all; on the way, back we stopped off at the butchers and there was a space right outside. I went in and had a look, I don't normally shop in a butchers because I like to know how much I'm spending and I'm not sure how much weight things will be. So, I had a look and spotted some ribeye steaks, my mum always raves about them, so I asked for two because they were huge, the butcher put them on scales,

"That's £15."

"Ok thank you."

In my head I was thinking, HOW MUCH??? That's why I don't like butchers (sorry butchers) I'd never have bought them if they'd have been priced up in a supermarket, the kids were made up though, because they were getting steak for tea!! When I got back in the van, Ella said that man's really staring at me; I said,

"It's because you look about 12, he's probably wondering how the hell you're driving this thing!"

Dressed up, with make-up she looks her age but she looks lots younger when she isn't and at that time she was only 20. Back at the campsite, we quickly got set up again and the kids got on the roof to see how far they could see; I finally went to pay. It was the brightest day that we'd had, so I sat outside reading, with a cider in my hand. I suggested that we pre-cook the food inside then finish it off outside on the BBQ, but no one seemed keen, so I set about prepping it all. If I say so myself, tea was gorgeous; steak, roasted peppers, onions, potato and mushrooms with a cream cheese sauce; the kids had the main steaks, while I had the bits cut off the end. Rather than turn the telly on, we played some rounds of HEADS UP, a kind of hi-tech charades on a phone, it's a very funny game; then the kids played scrabble, whilst I did a bit of reading. Then we did put the TV on to watch the Fast and the Furious 7, it's a great film of the franchise, made all the more poignant by the death of Paul Walker while they were making the film. It's so sad and moving, some of the things said just seemed weird knowing that he had died, there was lots of

action and special effects too so all in all an awesome film......
In other news, I had been jerking a lot, it's always a sign that
my body is over tired and that I was doing too much, it was
worth it though, time spent with the kids like this, I couldn't
miss out on.

Luckily the following day, we just chilled on the site,
playing games, reading and watching more of the Sons of
anarchy, because the weather wasn't great. That night was
the first night we'd needed any heating on, it wasn't really
cold but with it on for a bit, it was a little more comfortable. I
woke the next day at 10am and everything seemed to hurt, I
wasn't in a great mood along with the pain, I think that the
confined space and the kids noise was getting to me. I had a
shower and when I returned I'd had a missed call from Tes;
she'd been to collect a cheque for Ella and had seen a letter
from DVLA, so she had opened it and conveyed the BAD news.
Bad news can always wait ggggrrrr, I wasn't in a great mood
before, I could literally have screamed and cried all in the
same breath. Then in a discussion about jobs, Ella told me to
STOP FEELING SORRY FOR MYSELF! OMG I needed some time
alone. I knew that it was probably because I was just in a bad
mood but at the time I didn't see it that way.

Anyway, I went to do some washing up and decided to
have a nap, I had a good hour and a half and I felt better for it.
In the evening, we unhooked again and Ella drove into town
and we parked again, another lucky disabled spot on the end
of a run. I was just feeling wiped out, exhausted and my legs
weren't great either; Ella always senses this and lets me link
her. We went into the Mexican, Manana just in time, it was
only about 6.15 but already it was about half full, they were

turning people away not long after; busy, busy place with lots of families. The food was amazing, no wonder it was busy, I had fajitas and Jack finished them off after eating his. We had talked about going go for a drink but it was only Jack who really wanted to, despite it only being just after 7.45. So instead we got milk and got back to the van, drove back and hooked up, just before the rain came thundering down. Despite it being our last night I was happy to be back in the van, in the warmth, with a brew.

The following day we were going home, it had been a great week but hard work sometimes with the niggling the kids do, it does my head in; it made me think that it would be good on the cruise for us to do bits on our own so that we could let off steam. I was awake earlier than normal and as the kids wanted to get going, there wasn't any messing about; we were aiming for no later than 10am to set off, we actually got off for 9.40. Other days I hadn't even been up at that time; we made good time but it was busy. Again, Ella did really well driving until we heard some sirens from behind, us just as we were going into a restricted lane with cones down one side, she had no-where to go, to get out of the way to let the ambulance go past.

"Just pull in between the cones."

I had been allowed to sit up front, on the way home.

"Oh god it's right behind me!"

"It's ok don't stress, just pull over, if you damage one of the cones, you'll be ok because you had to get out of the way for the ambulance."

She pulled over through the cones, out of the way, to let the ambulance past and she calmed down again, we carried on with our journey; we arrived home about 12.30 and set about unloading the van. We had to take everything out, as it was the last time that we would be using it until the February, when we were due to go away again in it; Ella and I dropped the van off at the storage. Next, we went to pick up Charlie, he'd been at his second home with Elaine and her lot.

When I got back home I started feeling weird and dizzy, really off, I then realised that I hadn't taken my medication and it was 4pm; it just shows that I need the medication, I suppose. I started getting a headache next, I took some medication and lay down in my darkened bedroom. At the same time, the kids were getting ready to go out, I was looking forward to some peace and quiet. I started on the huge washing mound, but when I went to check on the second load of washing, something wasn't right, it was making an awful noise; so, I turned it off and I was keeping my fingers crossed that it would be all better in the morning, I was hoping the magic fairies would come and fix it in the night.

I went to bed early and was sleeping well when the phone rang, it was 3am! Ella had come home she had planned on staying at her friend Evie's house but instead she paid £40 to come home, she said she just wasn't feeling it, it worried me especially as she'd stood outside for about half hour before calling the house phone. Then as Jack wasn't in I text him and he was 'around the corner' but with no key! Kids eh?

Chapter 18

It's complicated!

A day later, I was sat ready and waiting for Joanna, as she is always on time or early and I was thinking oooohhh she's a bit late ...... then I realised, that I was in fact an hour early!! She picked me up on time, then we went to the cinema, we were watching the new James Bond film SPECTRE, which was great. I loved the locations, which were just beautiful and spectacular, it had a decent enough story and the action sequences as ever with a Bond film were amazing; the only thing I thought it could have had more of, was humour, but it was a small criticism. Once I was home we ordered a takeaway, me the kids and Jack's friend Aidan, there's rarely food left over because Jack and Aidan can eat! I was absolutely knackered, I couldn't seem to catch up with my sleep, I was ready for bed about 8pm, I finally turned the lights off at about 9.30.

The schools were all back in after the half term, so it felt like the first day back at work, despite me not actually having a job as such, for me it's more my routine; I wasn't really looking forward to it because I had things which really needed sorting. It was November and I'd still made little progress with setting up my online business, I had done a little research but nothing substantial, I had given myself some time off but it was time that I buckled down and got something done. One thing which I did do, was to contact the

ESA (Employment support agency) because I had barely any money coming in and they seemed to be dragging their feet, it seemed like all government agencies did! They were saying that apparently, I'd not filled in a particular form, which wasn't relevant because it was asking about the hours I had worked, when I'd not worked any at all, so effectively I wasn't being paid because I hadn't filled in a form, about work, which I hadn't done! Unbelievable, yet again!

I also sent yet another letter to the DVLA, I had already contacted the 'normal' office then when I wasn't happy with them I had made a complaint. When I wasn't happy with how they too, were dealing with the situation, I decided that I would write to the higher executive! You have to follow a strict protocol and go through each stage and I was really getting peed off with the whole thing. When you have had the freedom of being able to drive and then it is taken off you, it is just so frustrating; you can't just nip somewhere, you have to plan where and when you are going to do things and you have to rely on people all of the time. I felt that it was limiting my progress and I was still really cross about it.

To add to my frustrations the washer was still not working, I tried it again thinking that the magic fairies had been in the night but surprisingly it still wasn't working!! There was still washing in it, so I had a look at the washer and managed to drain the water out, making a mess in the process, but I did manage to get the clothes out which were heavy and dripping wet. With my 'engineer head' on, I decided that it must be something to do with the draining, I ran another empty load but it wasn't draining out again, so that confirmed my diagnosis. Tessa popped to collect the rest of the washing, as I had quite a pile and couldn't get it done, she got it done quickly, bless her and sent it back later in the day with Little Jo, who lives around the corner. Then I had three lots of wet washing to get dry because the weather wasn't on my side either, it was hung everywhere around the house.

I watched the film AMERICAN SNIPER, a moving true story; a dramatic film about a US soldier's tours and the effect on his home life. It's no wonder soldiers come back from war damaged and broken, the things which they see and experience and how they have to live their lives. It is an amazing film which will pull at heart your heart strings and regardless of your views on war it is a difficult watch, it shows how strong a person can be when they have no other choice. I love films which have a lasting effect on you, they leave you feeling more fulfilled and understanding somehow. I am a big film lover but I'm not into horrors, I am too easily scared, I was traumatised as a 14-year-old, I watched 'The exorcist' at my friend Terence's house. He was one of the first people with a video player, so we would watch lots of films there; but after the exorcist I had nightmares for about 6 months and even now it freaks me out. A few years ago, I went into the 'horror house' (I can't remember the actual name) at Blackpool, basically there are scary scenes with real actors and when we came to the 'Exorcist room' I lost it; I screamed and fell to the floor with my eyes closed because I didn't want to see anything, my friends had to come back and rescue me!

November 3rd, I had yet another doctor's appointment and this time it was Kim who had volunteered to take me, I had to have my bloods done first, I have them done every few months to keep a check on my levels. I'm not normally a good customer but the phlebotomists rarely have an issue, which I am thankful for. Next, I saw DR Smith, I didn't really have a regular doctor, I didn't mind because all the doctors were pretty good to be honest. I'd been asked to come and see the doctor because I had sent out a letter to all my doctors, a couple of weeks earlier because I hadn't seen any doctors for a while and because I saw different consultants who didn't know what the others were doing, I thought that I would send out a letter to everyone, which brought the information together.

'Anna Gray NHS no– XCXCXCXC'

14th October 2015

Copies to Mr. Sinha, Dr. Sharma and GP

Dear all,

As my appointments are some time off so I felt that ,I needed to contact you. With regards to my appointments I have an appointment with the joint endocrine clinic (seeing you both) on the 25th November but no MRI til February? Then I am due to see Dr Sharma on the 1st December; are both appointments needed?

I am writing with an update after seeing Dr Shultz on the 9th October – a junior doctor did the work up, which was very thorough (my 24hr urine sample results were missing from my doctors) and then she consulted with Dr Shultz. He explained that despite the change in my bloods etc. my kidneys have suffered no permanent damage and that it seems that the problem isn't primarily with my kidneys but he talked about seeing a specialist to explore an autoimmune disorder, which may explain the issues which I had had.

I am still extremely tired sleeping 10-12 hours at night plus I often take a nap in the afternoon which can range from 1-2 hours; the last few weeks this seems to have been particularly bad with dizzy spells and sickliness too, which had also been absent for some time. On top of the usual pains and aches in my hands and feet, I am also having additional pains in my knees and I now have areas especially on my heels where I have no feeling. My feet continue to be swollen too.

The junior doctor said that my blood pressure was high and may need to be monitored with a 24-hour monitoring test maybe? I am due to get my next bloods take on the 10th November – as I am getting my bloods done every 3 months, could it be possible to have a full work up to check my all my levels not just the renal? Also, I have been on the medication for the anemia for 3 months, does this need checking too, to see if it has affected my levels? With all of this in mind I wonder if there could also be an investigation into the growth hormone issue to see if that would help some of my symptoms?

I am not working now, as I couldn't cope with the tiredness, but I keep busy and I am exploring an online business, so that it gives me some flexibility in my work. I look forward to identifying and addressing these issues and I am doing all I can my end by eating extra healthy and generally looking after myself.

Thank you for your time and consideration, Anna Gray'

The issue which I had, seeing different consultants, was that they all dealt with their own area but there were symptoms which were causing me a lot of problems but weren't being addressed, so I was pushing the doctors to get things sorted because I was getting frustrated, I felt that I wasn't progressing as I should have been. So, I knew that my appointment with my GP would be interesting; firstly, he'd asked to see me for a double appointment to go through my letter, he listened but I'm not sure he got me and understood me, it didn't start well because when I mentioned my operation he asked 'Oh you've had an operation?' He didn't know me and when he was saying certain things, I was thinking that's not me. I got frustrated because he was saying that food and exercise balance will be the thing which puts on weight, which was true but he didn't seem to be taking into account the bigger picture. I explained that I was eating less and trying to be active but I'm in so much pain and have no energy that I was limited. I did add that I was on steroids which could make it difficult to lose weight, I seemed to have underactive thyroid which also made you put on weight and then there was the issue of my unaddressed growth hormone issue which also made you put on weight; I really was fighting against the odds!

I think then he thought he may have spoken a little out of turn, because he then backtracked a little saying 'I'm not saying it's your fault'. To be fair, he was sending me for more tests and was following other things up and he said YOU ARE COMPLICATED, I had to agree that I was but who else was I going to go to for help? Then he spoke about my serotonin levels maybe being low, and he was asking for me to think about whether I was depressed or not? He was referring to antidepressants, I have no issue with the use of antidepressants when they are needed but I didn't feel that I was depressed, so I didn't feel that I needed any, at that time anyway. I did say that I was getting angrier and I was pissed off at the situation and the lack of progress in general, so I said that I would think about it and speak with my consultants on the 25th. I was in with him for more than half an hour, so he was pretty thorough, I went home thinking about whether my mood was having more of an impact than I had thought.

I had yet another nap 3.30 till 5 and as usual I didn't want to get up once I woke, but I forced myself and sorted tea with Jack's help. We made home-made tomato soup, jacket potato and cheesy leeks; I only had the soup, a small bowl and only a little bread. I was determined that I was going to keep a check on what I was eating, to prove to myself that I was eating well. This went out of the window though when Ella,

232

who had been out with Katie, came back with McDonald's ice-cream for me!! The following day I got up determined, I was aiming to be even more active and watch what I ate, after what the doctor had said, I was 88.2 kg and I knew that it was way too much and it was affecting my confidence. I'd spoken to Jack and Ella about whether they thought that I was depressed and it was a resounding NO, I said you can be honest, Jack said,

"Well you get shouty sometimes but that's normal!"

"You do get frustrated with how things are, but I would say that that's understandable in your circumstance." Ella added.

The following evening the girls minus Elaine came for book club, we talked about lots and a little about books; Tor was struggling with her teenage son and we talked about how children changed when their hormones kicked in. It did make me think again that information and advice for parents struggling with their children or those parents who couldn't get the help they needed, for their own children; offering some help and guidance would be a great idea as part of my new business. Then I told them what the doctor had said and asked what they thought, they agreed wholeheartedly with the kids that I wasn't depressed. Tor said,

"You're about as far away from being depressed as you could be!"

"No, you're not depressed, you are surprisingly upbeat considering what you've been through, I'd be a mess."

Added Deb. Even though deep down I thought that I wasn't depressed it was reassuring to know that people close to me thought the same too.

Joanna's 40th birthday was coming up and the book club was clubbing together to get her something nice but I wanted to give her something personal too, so I was putting together a photobook for her. Pictures are so great for eliciting emotions and memories but since the age of the digital camera and phone cameras we don't print so many pictures. I had years of photos stored on a USB stick which I now can't find, which is awful, years of memories just gone, now of course we have the 'cloud' or similar which saves them somewhere, known only to a few!! Anyway, I made a book up of funny pictures and memories and it was a lovely task for me too because most of the memories were shared memories.

Ella had been stressing about telling her employers about her travelling, they had been so good to her that she felt really guilty about leaving. Then one day she came home for lunch and she'd spoken to her line manager because some other people were leaving and so her supervisor was concerned as to why they were. I think that it was just one of those things, but Ella ended up telling her that she too was leaving, she said that it was awful. If Ella could have split herself in two and carried on working and done the travelling, she would have, she doesn't like to upset people, she doesn't like confrontation but she did feel better now that it was actually done. It made it all seem more real, we had planned and talked about the possibility of travelling for so long and now things were falling into place. Again, Ella's work were great with her saying that when she was at home she had a job there, so for Ella it was music to her ears, it was more than she could have hoped for. She would travel for a month, then work for a month to pay for more travelling, it was the perfect scenario.

That afternoon, I had a man coming, to hopefully sort out the washer, he was an old school friend of Tessa's and came highly recommended. He took it all apart and worked while he talked, which is not a given with all workmen! He fixed it and it turned out to be a damn hair clip which had caused all the problems, luckily it was just £30, I didn't need the magic fairies after all!

Friday the 6th of November was my 'Graduation day', I had invited and paid for Jack, Ella, Tes and Kim to come along, mum and dad were in Spain. At first, I couldn't find the tickets and then I couldn't decide what I was going to wear. We set off by 11.30 and made good time and found a parking space, the ceremony was being held at Bridgewater hall in Manchester; we'd seen David Gray there a few years earlier, so we knew how impressive a building it was. I booked in and collected my tickets no problem, as it was busy we nipped out for a bite to eat and when I returned I collected my robes which cost about £50 odd, BUT NO HAT!? I felt cheated, I'd obviously not read the small print; but when you see all the graduation photos everyone has hats, so I had presumed that I would be getting one too!

Then, before we had to take our seats we had a photo session; I hadn't booked the official ones because I hated having my picture taken at the best of times, so I wasn't going to pay for it. We took our seats, me in the stalls with all the

235

other students and the rest of the clan in the circle. The ceremony was long; there were a lot of people collecting their certificates and there were also a few long-winded speeches too. I had decided that I didn't want to walk up on the stage with my crutch, so the walk up the few stairs and across the stage was a little perilous, but when I collected my scroll my little support group went mad and it did make me smile, I walked along the stage and gave them a little wave. Later, they all told me, that they had all filled up and maybe an odd tear was shed too, when I had walked on to collect my certificate. I had worked so hard for my degree and it felt good to be celebrating it. I put it on FB and it was lovely to get congratulations and good wishes, a little bragging once in awhile is acceptable, isn't it? I had managed to get a 2.1 and I salute all of those fantastically talented and dedicated students who achieve a first, because I know how hard I had worked for my 2.1.

The next day I could have done with a day of rest but there was a group of us going to see 'Hairspray' at a local theatre. We all; me, Ella, Tes and Macy, Elaine and her daughter Maddie, Debbie and her daughter Abbie and Joanna met up beforehand and had a lovely meal at a pub close to the theatre, Albert's corner. The food was lovely but it was a little bit hectic with nine of us competing to talk. On the way to the theatre we went into the market hall to get sweets but the stall had gone!? It had probably gone years before but none of us had noticed, so we ended up in Wilkinsons getting a pic n mix, for the show. The performance of 'hairspray' was amazing, truly brilliant performances; it was a production by a local company called Curtain Call productions and their shows are so good, really professional and polished. So, it was another great day.

The following day was definitely a chilled day but we still managed to do a roast between the three of us. By the Monday I wanted to get going with my business, so I rechecked my to do list and began ticking it all off but I felt like I had a mountain of things to get done but only enough energy for about 10% of it. Pain is one huge thing to deal with but the lack of energy is so frustrating and debilitating, I hate it, it varies slightly each day but there wasn't a day when I felt like I ever had enough. I needed to start to cut my cloth accordingly, I was trying but sometimes it just wasn't possible to live a 'normal' life with the energy I had. I think if you know there is light at the end of the tunnel, like when you know that once you have a particular operation, you will recover, you will get back to normal. The situation for me was more complicated, I knew that I would never be the same as I was 'before' but I was still hoping for more; more progress, more energy and less pain, less sleep. So, I couldn't see the light at the end of the tunnel, it just seemed like a never-ending road for me and that didn't help anything.

The next afternoon, Janice, Joanna's mum came around for a catch up, we had always got on well and she had time on her hands and so did I. We talked nonstop about lots of nonsense, Joanna is very much like her, it's weird how we pick up on so many of our parent's traits and views on life. Jack took her home across town with me as an escort instead of her calling for a taxi, when we got back Jack's friend Taylor arrived. I sat and listened whilst the kids and Taylor were gossiping like teens down stairs, it really made me laugh; I always thought that boys didn't gossip like girls but how wrong I was.

On the Tuesday, I had yet another blood test, I didn't take my medication until after I'd had my bloods taken, to see what my bloods were like without taking it. Kim took me again and waited whilst I had a flu jab done too. When I got home the postman had been and there was a letter from the DVLA chief executive, saying that they were looking into my case, I also had a letter from DVLA saying there were giving me my license. In the envelope, was my ACTUAL license but just for one year, then I would no doubt have to go through the whole thing again! How weird is it that something had actually happened now that I had complained? I was so, so happy that I could finally drive again, after four months not being able to, but I was still very frustrated by the whole situation and why it had gone on so long. Tes would have complained and got something done but in the end, I left it because I had other things occupying my mind.

The following day Jack was at work and he text saying that Bernie had passed away in the night, Terri had text him; it was awful news but what can you say? We all knew that she was gravely ill and had only a short time but that doesn't help when it actually happens. It was just so sad and we weren't that close to her; it's more that we knew of her journey because of Terri and because of the parallels with me at the beginning. Ella came home from work sobbing when I told her, she's a sensitive sole, not sure if it was because she's not really been through this before or because she's thinking what if it was me!? Jack came home later and he too was really upset; me and Els went up to him and we all hugged, it's not a regular occurrence because Jack says 'it's weird' but it was needed. Jack was struggling because he felt helpless, he wanted to be there for Terri, at a time like that but as he wasn't with her, it was just making a horrible situation even worse for him.

I'd cooked cottage pie for tea but none of us ate very much; while Jack went up to his room, me and Els cram watched the of Sons of anarchy to keep our minds occupied, but Ella couldn't stop crying. Then every time I logged into FB there was another heartfelt message for Terri and her family, there was such an outpouring of love and support for them. The following day Ella was sent home, she was still very upset and she just chilled for much of the day, she nipped to her dad's for a bit, for a change of scenery I think. Jack was off work and did little of anything; I just didn't know what to do to help them feel better, we talked about how harsh it was but most of the time we were just pretty silent.

On Friday the 13th, I had a call from the doctor's secretary saying that the blood tests which I had had, showed an issue with my thyroid – it was under active; it had been heading towards it for some time to be honest. It was typical that it was 'under active' it seemed that my whole body had become slow and lazy! It was a good job that I was able to take it all in my stride - a significant disorder with lifelong medication and I was just told over the phone by a receptionist.

'Symptoms of an underactive thyroid'

Many symptoms of an underactive thyroid (hypothyroidism) are the same as those of other conditions, so it can easily be confused for something else.

Symptoms usually develop slowly and you may not realise you have a medical problem for several years.

Common symptoms include:

- tiredness
- being sensitive to cold
- weight gain
- Constipation
- Depression
- slow movements and thoughts
- muscle aches and weakness
- muscle cramps
- dry and scaly skin
- brittle hair and nails
- Loss of libido (sex drive)
- pain, numbness and a tingling sensation in the hand and fingers (carpal tunnel syndrome)
- Irregular periods or heavy periods'

So, lots of symptoms which I already had; tiredness, aching muscles, pains in my hands, feet and knees, weakness in my lower limbs especially, dry skin and of course WEIGHT GAIN! I was hopeful that the medication would help with everything, time would tell. I would have to have a blood test in a few weeks, to see if the medication was working. I had also been taking vitamin D with calcium, vitamin C and I was beginning with evening primrose oil and garlic capsules, every bit helps! I was still wearing my PAIN bracelet, well anti pain, and I was going to measure and weigh myself, so that I had a form of reference before and after taking the levothyroxine for my thyroid. I'm keeping my fingers crossed that it will all help the weight issue, tiredness and pain.

Later on, the Friday, Children in need was on, after the week we had had it was more emotional than usual, we were in quite a state. On the Saturday, I met up with Lisa, normally I was thinking 'oh god how will I get there what are the kids up to etc.??' But I could drive! We had a catch up at hers first then nipped to Molly's tea shop in Nantwich, for food; I had a big breakfast but only ate about 2/3. It's manic at work for Lisa and we talked about her wedding dress, her nephews and of course, the wedding itself. After all the sorrow of the week it was a lovely tonic to be talking about such a positive event.

Chapter 19

Sunshine

Joanna was having a 'do' to celebrate her 40, it was on Saturday the 14th of November at Nantwich football club; Tes had done all the decorating and it looked fantastic, she'd done a great job. We were one of the first to arrive but it soon filled up; the book club girls were all there, we rarely went out, out so it was a rare outing. The noise I found hard to cope with, probably a bit of age thing on top of everything else. At these sorts of things, I really wished that I had the energy to dance more, as you can imagine I have always loved dancing but I only managed a couple of songs, if I did many more I would truly pay for it!! It was a really good night though and we had such a laugh. I could have come home at 11 but I didn't really want to miss anything, so it was nearer to 12, I was totally knackered and I knew that I was going to ache but it was worth it all. Elaine said a classic – Ella had got us all up dancing and was giving us instructions, she said,

"Ok the next chorus, we're gonna flick our hair!"

Elaine turned to me and said,

"Ella and her Jessica rabbit body are gonna kill us! We'll just look silly, we're nearly 50!"

Ella did indeed look like Jessica Rabbit, in a figure hugging red number and she did forget we weren't spring chickens, it did make me laugh though. Tes struggled to relax bless her, because she wanted everything to go smoothly but she did do such a brilliant job helping to organise it. When I went to bed I wasn't sure if it was the new medication or the small amount of alcohol I had drank but I was feeling ridiculously dizzy. When I woke the following morning I still felt really dizzy, I didn't know what had caused it but it had been months and months since I'd felt that dizzy. So, I spent the day doing very little other than watching TV in my pj's, reading and shopping online.

The week after, my friend Babs, had had a hysterectomy and she was at home, so I was going to visit her; she'd had the operation some two weeks before, she was doing well but she looked worn out as she had had trouble sleeping. Babs has always been good to me when I had been ill, when I had been ill years before and I hadn't been able to go out and drink, or even walk between pubs; she had driven to pick me up and she had dropped me back off. I loved her for it because otherwise I would have been stuck in far more, at the time many of my friends had little ones and were struggling to juggle their own lives. Now that she had had this operation and she hadn't been able to do things and she was in pain, she said that she now understood a little more of how I felt, because she had experienced it a little herself. It is difficult to explain how you are feeling and coping and she said that she had tried to understand but now she felt that she understood far better.

Ironically, I had a bad day the next day, I just felt tired and weary like I'd already used up my daily energy. I'd borrowed my sister's blood pressure machine and I took my

BP it was 153/80 but pulse was only 48? It didn't seem right I really did need to chase up the doctor about it, the trouble was that one of the functions of your hypothalamus, is to control your heart rhythm, so was that the issue?

'The hypothalamus responds to a variety of signals from the internal and external environment including body temperature, hunger, feelings of being full up after eating, blood pressure and levels of hormones in the circulation. It also responds to stress and controls our daily bodily rhythms such as the night-time secretion of melatonin from the pineal gland and the changes in cortisol (the stress hormone) and body temperature over a 24-hour period. The hypothalamus collects and combines this information and puts changes in place to correct any imbalances.'

I suppose looking at that list, there's no wonder that I was in such a mess, my tumour was attached to my hypothalamus and had damaged it, plus my brain surgery had further affected it, as did the course of radiation I received. I was off my food, which wasn't a problem I could have been off my food for months and my body would still have reserves! The machine was a wrist one and wasn't great but I decided that I would try it again later after I had had a nap, it was a good two hours, heaven, I just never want to get up. Once I was up, I sorted something for tea but I had no appetite to eat it. Ella had a tiny bit and Jack was out; I ended up with a bowl of cereal.

On Wednesday 18th I was going to have a 'reading', I have had different ones done over the years some brilliantly accurate and some dismally awful but I had avoided having one done whilst I was really ill because I didn't want some worse news. My friend Tor worked in a shop and there was a lady, Stella who rented a room upstairs and did readings, she came highly recommended so I thought that I would give her a try. So, this a bit of what she said,

'She said of my dad – he was stubborn, concerned, breathless, pain in the arse, presses buttons, patient, good guy, defiant, thinks he's right, only one way, HIS WAY!!'

Now anyone who knows my dad would say that this is an almost perfect description of him.

'Mum – a comedy duo the pair of them, social, wind each other up, bonkers, talks a lot, a bit nosey, she has grilling techniques, caring, do anything for anyone.'

I think that this a pretty accurate, some points more than others!

'And me – private, hold it in, don't like to talk about things, I brush myself off and carry on regardless, I take too much on, plus I need to watch my weight and my hypothalamus is f***ed!!!'

She went on to describe both Jack and Ella to a tee too! So, what she told me all rang true but it didn't really tell me anything which I didn't already know; I'm not sure what I was hoping for, maybe a hint at what my future may hold but I came away a little disappointed. Why do we want to know what is in store for us? Could we do anything about it if we knew anyway?

The following day, I woke feeling weary again and I was glad to have just a home day. I should have been meeting up with my friend Claire, but she couldn't make it at the last minute, I was disappointed because we hadn't meet up much and I missed her. It seemed to be getting harder to move in the mornings, I felt like I'd ran a marathon and my body was rebelling. The following day I'd put a chilli in the slow cooker for tea and yet again Ella was saying that she wasn't eating it, she'd done it quite a bit recently. Jack said

"Mum, she's doing that thing girls do ...."

"Ehh?"

"You know when they don't eat....."

He does make me laugh, I was a little concerned but I think that she was still struggling with the news of Bernie passing. I was going to the cinema to watch 'Mockingjay part 2' so I thought that I would watch part one in preparation. My problem is that I jump at the slightest thing and if I'm tired my body is jerking too, especially if there are lots of loud noises. Years ago, when I was about 17, I went to the pictures with a boyfriend, to watch one of the Mad Max films and I jumped that high at one bit that the seat folded back and I ended up on the floor! So, watching the film which was funny and jumpy too, made me jump at every turn.

The next few days I did very little, bits and bobs here and there; I use that term a lot, don't I? When the kids were younger I used to say I had to run 'errands', I'd be dropping something off at a customer or something. When Jack was asked at school, what I did for a job he replied 'she runs errands!' So, I spent many a day, doing 'bits and bobs' like; putting the washing on, paying bills, putting some food in the crock pot, so pretty menial tasks. On a rare occasion I would nip to the local Tesco express and get some 'bits and bobs', how does that cost £30? So, I tried not to go for 'bits and bobs', normally I did a 'big shop' and had it delivered to the house, then the kids would put it away, it was a lot less hassle than going shopping and in addition I wasn't tempted to buy extras either. I always had extra food in like pizzas and pasta, then if any of the kids friends stay there's alway enough food. My house has always been an open house for Jack and Ella's friends, when they were younger I liked to know where they were and it has just stuck. At the weekend, our house is often full of young people; it's like a mass counselling session. I spent some time with Ella and her friend Becky and she said that she always feels welcome at our house, it always has a warm feeling, isn't that nice?! We also have a note on our fridge that one of the friends wrote saying,

'Anna, (heart symbol) please adopt us.'

It was originally signed by two of the friends but now it has now been signed by lots of them, it does makes me smile, I am just grateful that my kids have such great friends.

On Sunday the 22nd November, I decided that I would have a last 'chill day' before I got started on something else, so I spent a couple of hours reading and just chilling. We had a roast, as we do most Sundays; Jack peels the veg, I put everything on when it needs to go on and keep an eye on things and Ella gets it all finished and dished up. We like a good thick gravy with our roast dinner, the sort that sticks to the veg; the worst thing about going out for a roast is the gravy, it's normally thin and there is little of it. One of Ella's friends, Tabitha was coming around so I took the opportunity to go up early and get out of the way so that they could gossip.

My back had really been bothering me, it wasn't something which normally gave me trouble, I'd done stretches and I'd rested it enough, but nothing seemed to be working, my Fentanyl patch wasn't keeping it at bay nor was the morphine either, I just hoped that it would subside as quickly as it had come. My legs had been weak too and I was still taking a nap most days, I'd hoped by now that there would have been some improvement but maybe I had to take the medication for longer? Or maybe it wouldn't help that much with the fatigue? Nobody seemed to have the answers for me. So, I had another day where more was left undone than was actually achieved, I was getting quite a to do list and it wasn't getting any smaller. I really struggled after 8pm to stay downstairs, I needed to come upstairs and to lie down and chill, I was becoming quite an expert at 'chilling' ie doing a lot of nothing! I needed to get stuck into my business maybe that's what I needed, a good shake up, something new to focus on.

On Wednesday the 25th, Tes was off to Spain with Macy to surprise mum and dad, she loves a good surprise and has done it successfully, many times. On a Wednesday evening, at mum and dad's camp they always have a quiz; so Tes had arranged for someone else to pick her and Macy up from the airport and take them to the campsite. Mum and dad stay for about 5 months or so on a campsite called, 'Camping Marjal, Guardamar Del Segura', it's about half an hour south of Alicante airport. As mum and dad sat doing the quiz, Tes and Macy went in and surprised them; and what a surprise they had. They would have a week there and then they'd be back a couple of days and I would be going, I was really looking forward to a change of scenery and hopefully a little sun.

My back had continued to trouble me so I booked in for a massage; Trina did reflexology first and then she did me a back massage. I had never expected to like reflexology because I hate, hate, hate having anyone touch my feet, it traumatises me when the kids try and tickle them, but for some reason I love reflexology. It relaxes me and it amazes me, what it reveals about your general health too. The back massage was ace too and she said that it may be sore for a few days and then should ease, it already felt better.

At the weekend Ella was off to Edinburgh to see her friend Nikki, who was at University there, but when they went to come home, their train had been cancelled because of the snow. She phoned an hour later to say that she had been caught in a snow storm, walking back to Nikki's place and was even more fed up, luckily, they were able to come home the following day because the weather had eased some. So, with

Ella away it was a quiet house and no mistake, I spent the day doing a few bits and bobs! Not a lot achieved but needed a chilled one in preparation because I was going out at night. It's like a military operation; I have a chilled day, I have a nap, I take extra hydrocortisone and I get showered, paint my nails and choose an outfit which hopefully doesn't make me feel too fat. Jack gave us a lift out, me and Joanna; we had three large rose wines and a spirit and I felt giddy. I even had a bit of a 'chair' dance, sitting down dancing, we had a good night and laughed a lot, I felt very merry, I hadn't many times since my operation. I got food but wasn't that fussed and Jack picked us up and ate half of it!

I got up the following morning and not surprisingly I felt a bit knackered and out of sorts I just thought that it was a bit of the effects from last night, I was getting all shaky and feeling very wobbly. I thought that I'd over exerted myself, that I would settle a bit after I took my afternoon medication. It wasn't until after my roast at 3.30 that I realised that I must have taken the wrong medication in the morning, instead of taking my morning medication I had taken my evening ones instead, so I'd not taken my hydrocortisone or levothyroxine. I often stop taking certain medications and supplements to see if they are actually working or not, I've done this with several things and sometimes it has no effect and other times I can tell that I have not taken it. Missing my hydrocortisone is a biggie for me.

Over the weeks I had begun to do a bit more about setting up my online business; I had a lot of literature which I had been going through to establish what was relevant and what I couldn't use, it took some time. I spent many afternoons and mornings gathering this information and deciding what resources would fit in with the groups which I was planning. I had done many different group sessions working with children in schools, addressing all sorts of issues; from behaviour to anxiety and alcohol to relationships so I had the basis for a number of groups. My plan was to devise group programmes which could be delivered by teachers or learning assistants; I wanted to use a seven-week delivery plan with each of the seven sessions having detailed instructions and guidance. Along with the detailed lesson plans, I wanted to produce worksheets for the students to complete too. So, there was a lot of work to be done before I was ready to put it on a website, I had done a lot of research and there wasn't a lot out there offering this type of service. I knew what I wanted with regards to the material and resources I wanted to use but in this age of modern technology I was stumped as to where to go for advice.

When I had run my business some 10 years before we hadn't needed a website and social media was unheard of, so this business would be a very different kettle of fish for me. I had an old dancing friend who ran a successful business, supplying office type workers, for small businesses, so I went to see Pam. She couldn't help me directly but she gave me a lot to think about and also gave me some contacts to get in touch with, to see if they could help me on the next stage of my business. I had had several productive days and I had gotten some things done but nothing substantial; best of all I had folders sorted for the business plus I went through all of my folders and info and either deleted it or reassigned it to a specific folder. I had decided on a core of programmes which I was going to work on, so before I began planning them, I wanted to organise all my information. I am very much a methodical worker and I need order to work at my best. I had some paper resources and some digital ones too and I needed to organise them all into digital versions for my programmes; I am not the most techie of people so this was a challenge in itself.

As I was setting up an online shop basically, I wanted to validate my worth and experience; so, I asked some former colleagues and students for testimonials and I had already had a good response. I enjoyed that part of the process because I was basically asking people to write something really nice about me, to big me up as much as possible. Some people who I asked never responded, so maybe theirs would have been not so favorable but we will gloss over that part and concentrate on good bits. So here goes with some blatant boasting,

From two former colleagues,

'I had the pleasure of working with Anna at Shavington High School during this time Anna conducted herself as a caring, hard working professional, always willing to go that 'extra mile' in order to secure the welfare of pupils in her care. She understands the importance of building good relationships with pupils in her care and is able to use her considerable interpersonal skills to great effect when working with youngsters who exhibit more challenging behaviours. - Neil'

'Anna has the ability to build wonderful relationships with even the most challenging of students. The impact of her work is seen through the fantastic results the students in her care produce (academically and emotionally) Her professionalism is second to none and I wouldn't hesitate to recommend her work to anyone. The results seen speak for themselves, and the young people (and adults) she works with have huge respect for her. - Katie'

From two former pupils I worked with,

'Anna Gray has been a massive part of my life. I have suffered with bad depression, anxiety and behaviour issues for most of my life and in high school Anna helped me through those times I struggled. I left high school in 2013 and to this day I still think back to how she helped me and what she would say to me now if I was to go to her with my issues. I learnt how everyone is fighting their own battles and every insecurity I had was mirrored in my classmates; it made me feel like I wasn't alone, it gave me the confidence to ask for help when I needed it. - Kris'

'The group sessions I took part in during my time at Shavington High School, have given me a good grounding in life now. I didn't get on as well as most and Miss Gray helped me think about the consequences of my actions, and helped calm me down and think logically about any situation I was in. She gave me so much direction, seeing potential in me that others, and even myself didn't, and I can honestly say this has given me drive and enthusiasm to achieve things that without Miss Gray, probably wouldn't even be an option for me right now. I truly looked forward to my sessions with her, they were a great help. - Oliver

As you can imagine hearing those sorts of things said about you are always nice to hear; I loved all of the responses but especially those from former pupils. One of the main reasons I first started working with children was in the hope of helping those who I worked with, even if the odds were often stacked against me. I am so happy when I see children I worked with and they tell me that they are doing well and are happy, it really is music to my ears. It was still the thing which I would miss most about working with children, the hope that what you are doing is going to help them be better, happier people.

I had had a telephone conversation with a lady who Pam had recommended, she set up websites and did marketing etc. She seemed a nice enough lady, but there were quite a few things which she would market out because she couldn't do them herself, which would be an extra cost to me. Plus, she lived about a half hour drive away. She'd explained, how to check if I could have the names which I wanted, so I spent time researching after the call for a name. The trouble was that I couldn't have all the ones which I had canvassed and asked people about. Then as I looked around my kitchen my eyes came upon my canvas, 'You are my sunshine', oooooohhhhhh. So, I couldn't do any of my original choices but I could do 'Sunshine groups', then I thought of a tag line of 'interventions for a brighter future', which fit really well with the purpose of the groups, so I was pretty happy about it.

I had lots of ideas about what to do with SUNSHINE (now the name of my new business) and things were constantly floating about in my head, I even had a notepad by my bed because it was keeping me awake at night too. I began to try and do some writing for SUNSHINE, in the mornings when my brain was fresher and it seemed to be paying off because I was chipping away at my long to do list. I sat on my sofa or at my desk with my computer and worked on the generic type worksheets which all the groups would require, but I needed a logo before I could go much further with the worksheets.

I finished the month on a positive note with a bit of a pamper day and I finally felt like my business was starting to take some shape too. I was going to Nantwich to meet my good friend Babs, my legs weren't great, I knew as soon as I got moving so I used my stick. We had a good catch up, Bab's friend Sally joined us too. Babs understands what I've been going through, so much more now that she's had her operation, bless her and Sally had been through breast cancer, so we made quite a group. I just had tea and crumpets. Then I went to Essence, a beauty spa, because I had booked in for a massage and eyelash tint. It was HEAVENLY, absolutely perfect!! It lasted nearly two hours, she massaged me and then she did the eyelash tint; so rather than getting up after I had been massaged, I could just lie there, enjoy and relax. I loved it. It was lovely to have my muscles eased and relaxed, I did feel a little like I was cheating on Trina but I had been given a gift voucher!

Chapter 20

Nap, Nap, Nap

December 1st! I was having my van serviced so I had to go and get it, it's great that it is in a secure lock up but a flippin pain when you have to unlock and lock everything going in and coming out. But I wanted the van serviced and safe for all our trips away, my mechanic Graham is great, I can really trust him. If Graham says that I have to have something done then I know that I need it doing. He comes to the house which is a bonus too because while he was working, I could get on with others things. Graham serviced the van and he said that I'VE GOT A REALLY GOOD VAN it's in really good nick, it seemed to be a unanimous opinion, dad and Harley had said the same thing. He also recommended a solar trickle charger for the battery, so that I didn't have the same issues again, so I Googled it (how did people cope before Google?) and I managed to get one from eBay.

I had a call from the Walton hospital, wanting to bring my appointment forward but it would have been when I was on the cruise; so, we agreed to leave it and swap the MRI until when I get back from the cruise too. I wasn't symptomatic from the tumour, as in I wasn't getting the really bad headaches, so I didn't believe that it had grown, so I figured another couple of weeks or so would be fine. The next day I was up early to get my injections done for the cruise, neither Jack nor Ella needed any, because apparently those which they'd had already, covered them. When I went into the room, the nurse said,

"I had to call an advice line about you, you are a pretty complicated case."

"That's not the first time that I've heard that!"

"Well judging by what I've read, you deserve a holiday."

"Well this year I have had holidays around all of my appointments, next year it will be holidays booked in first and appointments fitted around them."

"I don't blame you."

I had to have two injections and as the nurse had said that it would be sore I elected to have both injections in one arm, so it was sore!! However, we had quite an emotional day ahead so became insignificant, it was Bernie's funeral. We left early, so that we'd get a space, as we knew that it would be busy, she was such a lovely, popular lady. It was such a beautiful service, we all cried, I tried to remember all the Catholic responses from my childhood and I sang badly. The church was full, so many people had turned up to show their respects. We went on to the wake after, to pay our respects to Terri too, again it was busy and we didn't know whether we should be there or not, we stayed until we'd spoken with Terri and we left shortly after. Funerals are such a saddening thing but they do make you value your own life and hug your loved ones a little tighter too.

On our way home, we called in at Tesco and spent my bonus points on a load of new Christmas decorations, it had been a while since we had had any new ones. I was gob smacked at how expensive they were, but it was fun, we all chose our own pieces and it was a good counter balance to the sadness of the day. Then when we got home, we got the rest of our decorations down and we put them all up around the house. I do love the house when it is all dressed for Christmas, it makes the house seem magical somehow, it's a pain putting them up and getting them down again but we have our money's worth of pleasure in between. It had been a long day and by the time we watched I'm a celebrity, I was tired but surprisingly not as exhausted, so I do think that the tiredness is easing, HOORAY!! at bloody last. (this was short lived!)

My legs weren't great when I went to bed and I was woken about an hour or so later with severe restless legs and pain; so took some medication and eventually I dozed off again. I woke some time later, when I heard Ella moving about, I assumed that it was morning but it was 5am and Ella was being violently sick. So, she had to have the Thursday and Friday off work because her work rules say that once they had been sick they had to wait 48 hours before they could come back in. She works in a nursery and so there are a lot of germs flying about and they do it to minimize everyone catching the bug as much as possible. She was a bit annoyed as she had her work's do on the Friday, she would have to miss that too as a result, poor thing she'd missed the one the previous year because I was in hospital. Bless her, like me she hates being sick, so I was up and down 'supporting ' her whilst she was being sick; she just wanted me there she wouldn't let me go. I wasn't really doing anything I was just a bit of moral support I think.

My doctors called, they had received the letter from Dr. Shultz which I had received about a week or so earlier, they needed me to come in for an appointment and to discuss some more tests. They were talking like it was an urgent affair, despite the fact that I saw the consultant two months before, so it could hardly be that urgent. They said that I had to go in and speak with the Doctor, to go through the as it was three pages long and complicated. Unfortunately, I was seeing the man who didn't even know that I had had an operation; I was thinking, I'll know more than him! Below is an excerpt from the letter,

'Her most recent eGFR is 62mls/min, putting her in the normal range category. Her urine dipstick showed a trace of blood, 1+ protein and ++leucocytes. Unfortunately, the 24-hour urine collection results were not available on ICE because Mrs. Gray lives out of the area.'

The remainder of the letter just went on about my history and basic descriptions of what the consultant had examined, so really nothing to be getting het up about. In preparation for my appointment with the doctor, I reorganised my blood results as they were becoming a little jumbled; it is easier to discuss things when you have all the information at your finger-tips. Unfortunately, the appointment was USELESS! First off, he hadn't even read the letter, he knew nothing about it, unbelievable! I'd already gotten a copy of the letter from reception before my appointment to confirm that it was the same one that I had received, there was nothing particularly significant in it, I really didn't know what the fuss was all about. Again, it was a good job that I was on top of my game and that I knew what was going on, otherwise I'd have been in a right mess; I acknowledge that I am a complicated case, but surely reading my notes is a good start?!

December the 4th, IT'S BEEN A YEAR TODAY!! A year ago, I was tearful and by 10.00am I was under the knife! A lot had happened in that year but if truth be told, I did think that I would be further down the path of recovery, I still wasn't prepared to accept that how I was feeling was as far as I was going to get. One big thing which had changed was my focus, I was determined that 2016 would be all about new experiences and holidays; it was not going to be ALL about doctors and appointments. I hated being the ill one and I just needed to push myself to move forward in some way or other. I had made the decision to make 2016 my best yet.

I had a dentist appointment but I was done by 11, I was going for brunch with Joanna's mum, so I picked up Janice and went to Frankie's and Benny's because they do a mean breakfast. I had a big breakfast and it was yummy. We talked non-stop; Janice regaling me with all of the stories of her younger self. Each generation thinks that we created 'rebellion and youth' but that's just because parents don't want us to know everything that they got up to, when they were young. There are things that I am still finding out about my mum and dad and my kids don't know half the stuff I got up to, I'm not sure they ever will!

Jack came home and wanted to talk, he'd been thrown by recent events, so he'd asked his friend Sam over to talk. So, we all had an input about what he should do and how he should do it, but he still wasn't sure what he should do. Somehow the conversation got onto how women change their minds and boys never know what they are thinking, so I gave Sam THE RULES to read,

1. The FEMALE always makes THE RULES.
2. THE RULES are subject to change at any time without prior notice.
3. No MALE can possibly know all THE RULES.
4. If the FEMALE suspects the MALE knows all or most of THE RULES she must immediately change some or all of THE RULES.
5. The FEMALE is never wrong.
6. If the FEMALE is wrong it is due to an unavoidable misunderstanding which was the direct result of something the MALE said or did.
7. The MALE must apologies immediately for causing said misunderstanding.
8. The MALE is always wrong.
9. The MALE may be right if he agrees with the FEMALE unless she wants him to disagree.
10. The FEMALE may change her mind at any time.
11. The MALE may never change his mind without the express written consent of the FEMALE.

12. The FEMALE has every right to be angry or upset at any time.
13. The MALE must remain calm at all times, unless the FEMALE wants him to be angry and/or upset.
14. The FEMALE must under no circumstances let the MALE know whether she wants him to be angry or upset.
15. The MALE is expected to mind read at all times.
16. If the FEMALE has PMT all THE RULES are null and void.
17. The FEMALE is ready when she is ready.
18. The MALE must be ready at all times.

Sam's response was,

"Well that's not fair."

"Welcome to the real-world Sam."

I think that he thought that it was a real list, not a mickey take!

I was going to the airport early the following morning, to fly and see mum and dad in Spain, so I was in bed for 10. I'd set my alarm to wake me but a notification which bleeped woke me; I ignored it at first but then I checked and it was 3.31am and I had set my alarm for 3.30. It hadn't been my alarm going off, the beep had been an email, so I was very lucky that I did actually look at my phone. It was really blustery out. When I get up at odd times I never know when to take my 'morning' medication, some could wait but if I didn't take my hydrocortisone I could feel really dizzy and sick; so, I took that on my way. I went through security, I'd paid for a 'fast track 'pass but because I had a crutch they ushered me through anyway. I went to the toilets to sort myself out and to put on my sexy circulation socks, I'm not sure if I needed them or not but I just thought that they can't do any harm. I bought a couple of drinks because I am always thirsty in the morning and they are far more expensive on board and I waited for my flight to be called, I never rush when a flight is called because you end up standing and waiting ages to board anyway. I'd paid for priority but they'd already started boarding 'normal' passengers by the time I arrived, typical, but it meant that I didn't have to queue at least. A man helped with my suitcase and rather than watch a film I managed to have a nap, which was lovely, I had a good hour and a half maybe two hours.

Mum and dad sat waiting for me to come through, it's always big hugs all round and then a short journey back to their camp to unpack. They have a big caravan with a huge awning, which is set up for their five-month stay, they have two single beds in the caravan and a dining area which converts to a double; I was having dad's single and he was sleeping on the double because he stayed up way later than me. We sat and had a brew and a catch up but after about an hour or so I was wilting, so I had another good two-hour kip. I spent the afternoon catching up with all the different people who popped in to say hello and we had prawns and mussels for tea which was lovely, dad always does mussels when we go because he knows that we love them. We settled later to watch STRICTLY, I had a treat of hot chocolate with Baileys plus a brownie, after all I was 'on holiday'. By 9.30 I was ready for bed again. I kept waking up in the night thirsty and in pain, maybe because my meds were confused by the early start and long day?

The following morning, we were off to the other site, there is a sister site inland, as there was a car boot sale going on. It wasn't that busy but we met a few people and a lady who organises travel trips for the caravan club, so I planned to tap into her knowledge for our adventures. We just had a drink at the bar then we called for tapas at a little place on our way back. A big party came in, all dressed up probably just because it was a Sunday, it's a big family day there, I think they value the family unit more than we do here in old Blighty, which is a pity. Home and I decided on having a nap so that I wasn't in bed by 9pm. I had a good two- hour kip which was very lovely, but as ever I never want to get up afterwards, I forced myself to, so that I wouldn't miss out on tea. I watched some telly but I still only managed to stay awake till 10pm, but it was ok, I was 'on holiday'.

My mum and dad's site is a really nice and well-equipped site, there's a gym, an big outdoor and an indoor pool, plus there is a huge hydrotherapy pool. I was up for 10am and off to the hydro pool with dad, which I love, to see if it would help to ease my aches and pains. In the afternoon, I did a little reading outside in the sun, I had a nap and then for tea, we went going to the local Bodega with some friends of mum and dad's, Carol and Keith. When mum and and dad first started going to the Bodega it was more like a workman's cafe, mum and dad found it on one of there bike rides and we have been going ever since, but now there are as many 'campers' as workman who use it. We had a great time, the food is all home-made and it was delicious, plus as ever, lots of laughs. Dad gets his wine from there by the litre, I think he has the bargain basement one, which is about one euro or so a litre, he takes a 5 litre container and fills it.

The following day it was 11 before I decided to get changed, I think mum and dad thought that they had a teenager back in their 'house'. Every month on site , there is a 'ladies luncheon' and I happened to be there for it; so at lunch me and mum went up to the bar and there was about 20 plus of us and we sat outside for a bit in the sun until it was time to go inside to eat. We were seated at two large tables and it was a lovely help yourself buffet and free wine too, we had a fair bit of both! Afterwards we sat outside again, drinking and putting the world to rights, a few hours later the men returned from their jaunt and the drinking continued. I spoke to lots of different people; some old faces, some new, one couple were travelling Europe for a year, others who were there just for a month or so. The camp in the 'Winter season' is a real mix of people; ranging from those who have retired early, regulars, those who stay most of the year, and there are different nationalities too and everyone mixes at the various events they have going on

The next day was a lovely sunny day and we'd booked the use of an electric bike for me to use, to see how I fared, after how badly I'd done on a conventional bike I knew that an electric one would be worth a try. Electric bikes are expensive so I wanted to see how I fared on one before I invested in one; so once Colin, who's bike it was, had lowered the seat for me and given me some basic instructions dad and I, set off, poor dad was just on a normal bike. To avoid the main road, we went the back way, which is bumpy and full of holes and dips plus the odd sharp bend. The bends I struggled with because my balance and coordination were off and the bumps meant that I gripped that bit tighter so my hands hurt more. You have to cycle to kick in the electrics and my legs hurt especially my outer thighs but like I said to dad I can cope with the pain if it means that I have some freedom and I can get about easier when Ella and I went on our travels. When we got back, we had a nice lunch, then had another two-hour nap because Wednesday night was quiz night, so we all went up and teamed up with Jeff and Maggie, more friends of mum and dads. It's always quite a challenging quiz, I do love it, we never win, but it was fun taking part.

The next day I had another trip to the hydro pool, on my own, I do love it is so relaxing. For lunch we were going out with Kathy and Harley (mum and dad's neighbours there) to Chema, a lovely restaurant in Guadama. It was a very modern, all white restaurant, very different from most of the others and the food was gorgeous; we had another great afternoon. Kathy and Harley are great company and mum and dad were on top form, we stayed well into the afternoon. As we didn't get in till late, I had a nap later than normal, by this point I'd just given into having a nap whenever I wanted, after all 'I was on holiday'! When I got up, I went through some Spain stuff with mum, they'd done a lot of travelling over the years, so I wanted her opinion on where to visit, so that I could start to detail a bit more our plans for when we came to Spain.

The following day I did some more research on campsites from an ACIS book which Kerry, another friend, had brought round, I wanted to start getting some ideas together of where we should visit and where the best places to camp were. In the afternoon, mum and I nipped to Norma and Brian's caravan, because Brian had done his family tree and it had been printed in a book. Me and mum have done a lot of research on our family trees, it takes hours and can cost a bit too, but it is fascinating to do and very eye opening. We'd been told that we had 'people from the big house' in our history, well from the looks of it, it may have been the master of the house and a maid!! Brian's ancestry book was fab, really detailed and clearly laid out, he showed us some techniques and tips, the trouble is when you are doing research of this type you have to be a little flexible because often people would just say their names because they couldn't write, so often names were written down incorrectly or the scribe had poor handwriting.

When we got back to our van just before 4, I said that I was going for a nap, mum said,

"You're not going to have another bloody sleep, are you?!?"

"Yes, why mum? What's the problem, I'm doing noone any harm? You were saying to people at the ladies' lunch that I was always sleeping, I really don't understand what the issue is."

Granted, I did sleep a lot, 11 hours at night plus another couple in the day, it wasn't like I was lazy there were lots of reasons why I needed the extra sleep, it wasn't like I was doing it to spite anyone, it just was what it was.

December 12th, Macy's 11th birthday today and it was my last day; we nipped to the market and I bought Jack a belt and Ella a lipstick, I didn't normally buy pressies but I saw the belt and I had to get Ella something, I couldn't get one without the other. Back at the van and I was wilting again, so I had ANOTHER nap for a couple of hours. I then went next door to see Harley (Kathy was out) and I went through some questions about travelling because they too, had been to a lot of places and were knowledgeable and I was hungry for any information. The next day w,e were up early, for me anyway, and we were off to the airport by 8.30am, I felt sickie, I always do on travel days, I think that it's because you need an extra kick of adrenaline and I don't have the extra kick!? Big hugs good bye because we wouldn't see each other for another four months. My flight was delayed 'due to too much traffic over France', honestly!! I even managed to get a nap. I hate the journey back, because you just want to be home, don't you? A lovely lady porter, helping a man in a wheelchair, helped by ushering me into the lift so that I didn't have to use all the stairs. Then a grumpy man, who had just had a go at the lady in front of me, let me through to the front of the passport queue. Plus I had a good run home, I had no nasty letters to return to and I would be sleeping in my own bed, so a perfect end to a great week.

Chapter 21

The accident

December the 14th was a big day, I finally booked our ferry to Spain, we had decided to go on the long ferry to Bilbao, Spain, rather than drive all the way through France. Mum and dad did this so we thought that it was a good option, we would be on the ferry for nearly 28 hours, so we had a cabin booked too. Our D day was the 20th of February 2016, until I booked I think that I was still unsure whether it would actually happen so I was beyond excited. It was momentous for another, more trivial issue too; I have a favourite place to sit, we have two big sofas, so there is plenty of other available places to sit, but the kids would often sit in MY seat just to wind me up, I think. Well this morning it was Ella, but I fought her for it, she finally gave way when I lay on her and she couldn't move and was struggling to breathe; it was hilarious, I haven't normally got the strength to fight her off but this time my weight was actually an advantage for me!

The following day, Shaun, Elaine's husband was coming to do some jobs around the house and to fit a safety handle thing, on the van too. I was up early because he was due to come at 8.30 and I was normally still in bed at that time. He arrived about 8.45 and soon after I went off to collect the van. One of the five doors on the first floor was damaged and Shaun had come to see if he could mend it or if it needed replacing, he took one look and said that it did need replacing.

We discussed the other doors too because as they were old doors, it was unlikely that we would get a match, so I eventually decided on having all new. We also discussed the two doors which led into the living room, they had glass in the top section and did need replacing to fit in with the rest of the doors, but in the end, I decided that these could wait until another time. He was struggling with the tap which needed attention too and the van handle lock, which had come with incorrect fittings, nothing goes smoothly does it?

While Shaun was busy, I was booking the first-class lounge at Manchester airport and the meet and greet car park for when we went on the cruise. I took the van back and trudged through traffic to meet the SSC girls at the Duke of Gloucester a local pub, it was easy for us all to get to. We had a lovely bite to eat and a well overdue catch up, everyone was doing pretty well, which is good and not the norm; in a group of people there always tends to be at least one, who is having a tough time. We don't get together that often but when we do it is a mammoth session, three hours! By the time I got home it was nearly 8.45 and I was knackered, so I went straight to my room. It was a mess upstairs with doors off and bits of furniture misplaced, I just kept my fingers crossed that Shaun could crack on the next day and get them all fitted.

The following day Shaun made slow progress it seemed, but it's a big job fitting five doors especially with limited space and one door a heavy-duty fire door. I cracked on doing some SUNSHINE work, I'd done more than I'd realised, but I still had a plenty to keep me occupied for weeks maybe months. Shaun managed to fit the van handle lock because he had got some other fittings to use, he sorted the leaking taps and hung all the doors, he didn't finish until 8pm bless him. They needed a lick of paint but they looked really good and I was just glad that it was finished, I love Shaun but I don't like having men working at the house it makes me nervous and I just can't relax.

On December 17th, I had my follow up appointment at the Royal Liverpool, I had to be weighed, have my height measured and a sample taken too by the nurse. It was literally an empty waiting room, I had had to drive because no one was free to come with me, so I was very tired and had to really concentrate on what I was doing driving in. When I went into the room it was a new consultant, I didn't know where Dr. Sharma was; the new guy didn't start well,

"You're not a diabetic?"

"Errr no."

"This is a diabetic clinic."

"Right, I was told to come here, that's what it says on my letter."

Luckily, it did get better and we used all of my notes and muddled through because he seemed to have very little information at all. He said that I needed to have a bone scan done, because taking steroids long term can adversely affect your bones, so he just wanted to check how mine were, as I'd been on steroids for nearly three years at that point. He wanted me to have another insulin stress test done in a few months' time, to see if my growth hormone hadn't miraculously started working again; previous tests had shown that I had no growth hormone.

'Adults with growth hormone deficiency may have a wide range of symptoms. When these symptoms are severe, they can reduce people's ability to function – both socially and professionally – and this can dramatically lower the quality of their lives. These symptoms include:

- decrease in the amount of muscle bulk and strength.
- increase in the amount of fat in the body (especially around the waist)
- abnormalities in the amount of 'good' and 'bad' cholesterol. This can lead to an increase in the risk of heart disease.
- abnormalities in the blood and in the circulation.
- Osteoporosis.
- low energy levels and decreased stamina.
- impaired concentration and memory.'

My thyroid needed to be stable before they would even consider looking at my growth hormone, looking at the list of symptoms though, my lack of growth hormone could very well be the cause of many of my symptoms. One big concern about giving me the growth hormone, was that it can promote the tumour to grow and as I still had a tumour, this was something which would have to be taken into account when discussing whether I should be put on hormone replacement.

'Adult-onset growth hormone deficiency is treated with growth hormone replacement treatment. The growth hormone that is used is an artificial preparation that individuals can administer themselves. This is done using daily injections underneath the skin into the fat tissue around the lower abdomen, with an injection device. The needles are the same as those used by people who inject insulin for diabetes and the injections are virtually painless. Treatment starts as an outpatient with education and support, usually from an endocrine nurse. Once started, individuals are carefully monitored and given regular blood tests. The dosage of the growth hormone is adjusted depending upon the patient's response and results of blood tests.'

It wasn't something which I wanted to do but if it meant that I could get back to having a more 'normal' life, it was something which I would do; I wasn't sure how they would know if it would affect the size of my tumour though, if it started growing because of the growth hormone what then? Once I was done I went off to meet Sheila, she lives near the Gemini retail park in Warrington; we meet at M & S for drinks and a catch up. We had a lovely natter, Sheila had finished work and was adjusting to her new life and trying to make sure that she didn't get fed up sat at home, she is just such a social person that she needed to be around people. We talked about how our lives were going and our loved ones too, Sheila is in a similar position to me and she understands some of my frustrations about not being able to do things, so it was good to talk things through.

The following day, I had a very chilled one, after my busy week, I needed it, I did do some work on 'Sunshine' which I actually loving. I also spoke with another website designer, who had been recommended to me, on the phone he seemed very affable and rather than just saying 'yes I can do this and that' he said, 'have you thought about this?' This would be good for you?' This is the email I sent before our conversation.

'Hi Jamie,

I'm wondering if we could have a conversation over the phone, are you available tomorrow say about 11?

I can explain a little more of where I'm up to etc. I am not at the point of having all my material ready to go so to speak but I need some info regarding logos and names etc. to go forward.

I'm not sure what Tracey told you about my position but I have had a rough few years with illness and so this year I plan to do as much travelling as I can; which is one reason I chose an online based business. However, this will mean that I am limited with available meet up time.

Despite all this I would ideally be looking to launch say April for the new tax year if that is do able.

Thanks Anna '

His business was based locally and I liked the fact that he would be an idea's person too, plus the things which I needed with regards to logos and designs he could do rather than market them out; so I decided on Jamie, rather than the lady I had spoken to a few weeks before. So, I had had a productive day in many ways. At night both Jack and Ella were going out to Nantwich drinking, Ella's friends came to 'pre-drink', this is not something I ever did as a youngster, but they drink before they go out, then they go out later and they don't drink so much when they are out, so they save money! They were literally going out as I was going to bed, I can't go off before they go because apparently, I have the best mirror in my room, so everyone comes into use it! I went off to sleep and sometime later, about 3.30, I woke, I always seem to wake before the kids come through the door which is odd, they are always respectful and quiet but I'm nearly always awake first anyway. So, I was nodding off again, when I heard an awful noise, then screams and what I thought was that I had heard the door bang and that Charlie had somehow escaped. Then Ella was yelling,

"Mmmmuuummmmm!!"

I ran to the top of the stairs because it sounded like an urgent call and I stood at the top, in my pants and top and couldn't believe what I was seeing. Ella was stood with her left arm in the air and her right hand holding it and blood, the blood was all down her arm, I'm not the best with blood but I ran down the stairs. As I got to the bottom Ella's friend Becky was there wrapping tea towels around her arm, but they didn't cover all the cuts, in a whispered tone I said,

"Becky, I think we need another towel."

On Ella's left elbow there was a 4" gash, which was open a good half an inch or more. What I wanted to say was,

"OMG, EEEUUUURRRRKKKKKK." Instead I said,

"Ok let's get you sat down."

I went into the living room and Ella's friend Ellie, was already on the phone to get an ambulance; but she was being asked questions she couldn't answer, so she passed me the phone. Ella was now sat down with Becky, who was holding her arm up and trying to calm Ella down.

"Is the patient conscious?"

"Yes."

"How old is the patient?"

"20."

The questions seemed never ending, I know they have to ask certain things but I was getting impatient.

"Please can you just send an ambulance!!"

"An ambulance is on its way; these questions won't hold up anything."

Meanwhile Jack had come down, wondering what all the fuss was about, Ella wanted him to hold her hand but he wasn't fussed, and Ella kept asking,

"Am I going to die?"

"No, you will be fine, just stay calm." Answered a very calm and collected Becky.

Ellie had already started cleaning up, it was only then that I noticed all the glass on the floor and all the blood too. I didn't know what had happened but looking around it looked like she had gone through the glass in the door, the door which I had decided NOT to replace only a few days before!

"Jack, you go out front and keep an eye open for the ambulance."

"How many cuts does she have?"

"Quite a few, one is really big."

"Is there blood squirting?"

"No, but there seems a lot but there's no squirting."

"Mum I'm scared."

"I know, it will be ok."

"I'm so sorry."

Just then the paramedics came through the door and took over, they very calmly took off the towels and dressed the wounds to keep them clean. Ella just kept saying,

"I'm so sorry."

As soon as they had bandaged her arm, they said,

"We'll need to take her now."

"Ok I'll follow in my car."

"No mum, please come with me."

"I can't, if I come in the ambulance we won't be able to get home, it's fine I'll be there when you get there."

"Oh, Jack I need some trousers and a jumper!"

I was still in my pants and little vest top! He brought a pair of pyjama bottoms which luckily looked like joggers and an old jumper, but I was past caring. I drove and parked up and the ambulance had just arrived, the lady paramedic said,

"If she says sorry one more time!"

Apparently, she had continued to apologise all the way there, I suppose it was better than being abusive. Luckily, because of the alcohol in her system probably, Ella didn't seem to be in a lot of pain, so maybe she was lucky that she hadn't done it sober. We were taken to the waiting room and told that there would be a wait because it was 'mad Friday' or something, basically the worst, busiest day in the A and E calendar. We arrived about 4.30am and we sat waiting until

8am before we were seen. Normally when I have to take one of mine to A and E, I go prepared with drinks and snacks and maybe even a book, but there hadn't been any time, so we had nothing at all. We were both struggling to stay awake but there was plenty of people watching to be done and guessing why they were there!

We were taken through to minors and a nurse came and said that we needed to get Ella into a gown and she couldn't have anything to eat in case she had to have surgery, at this Ella's face dropped, because of where the big cut was she couldn't really see it. Ella said that her foot hurt and it turned out that she had some glass in it, the nurse helped her off with her jeans but none too lightly and caught her foot and Ella screamed out. The nurse said that she was lucky that it wasn't her face, when we told her what had happened and that it hadn't damaged any veins, but she had to have X rays on her arm and foot to check that there wasn't any glass left in, luckily she was clear.

After, the nurse had a look at the bandage and said that because we had had to wait the blood had dried to the bandages and stuck to her arm, so it would take a little time to get them off. She called for reinforcements and the two nurses began to soak the bandages in a solution and then they began to gently peel them off her arm as they. It must have taken a good 20 minutes to do, during which time had Tes turned up with Ella's mobile and some supplies, she's is a star at times like that; she said that the girls had said that Ella had just lost her balance taking her shoes off, of all things. Once the bandages were off Ella said,

"Mum take a picture."

"We'll ask the nurse when she comes back."

The nurse had gone for some more supplies, I didn't want to look at it never mind focus on it. I asked one of the nurses but they said that they weren't allowed to, so I had to man up and take a few pictures, it really wasn't a pretty sight. She sat there with this great big gash on her arm, posing for pictures!! She had a few little cuts and a few where the top layer of skin had been ripped off but there wasn't anything to be done with them. There were two other cuts which looked pretty bad, 1.5 inches long and open a good 1/2", I thought that they would need stitching for sure but they were just sterile stripped them, flippin amazing stuff and a skilled nurse to boot. The big cut had to have seven stitches, plus lots of sterile strips too, I reckon about 10 to hold it all in place, then she had a dressing put on and a bandage over that to protect it and to stop Ella moving her arm too much too.

We were done for about 11am, it had been a long night, I drove us home, we were both tired and stressed and Ella was feeling very sorry for herself by this point. Shortly after, Mark, Ella's dad, popped round and gave her no sympathy; he just took the mickey out of her but there was no malice in it. I did bacon butties all round and I had another cup of tea. I was in a mess with my medication but I felt that in the circumstances I needed another 5mg hydrocortisone at least. At 12 Tes called to take Jack out for a GOLF drinking game, with his football mates; someone had devised a game where they went from pub to pub and they had to drink a particular drink in each of them. Kim, Macy and Ant called briefly and then me and Ella just chilled and watched a film.

It was STRICTLY FINAL night, so I was determined to stay up and watch it, Ella had napped on the sofa but I hadn't managed to get a nap in. I was getting very restless so I took some medication about 8pm and I was feeling knackered, I was generally in a lot of pain probably from sitting in hospital chairs for hours, they aren't the comfiest for anyone and obviously the lack of sleep wasn't helping either. When we did go to bed, I made a bed up on my floor for Ella, her bedroom is on the second floor and up some difficult stairs, so I thought it best. In the end Ella slept in my bed and I volunteered to go on the floor as I was worried she'd fall or I'd tread on her in the night. I was desperate for a good night's sleep but as we all know things don't always go to plan. I was woken at 3.30am by a loud knocking on the door, I went down and it was Jack; oh dear lord, he stood there with a big grin on his face, I was not amused. He tried to go into the living, probably he was on his way to the kitchen but I knew that if he did I'd never get him upstairs, so I guided him up the stairs, but getting him up there was tough, he kept stopping and turning around asking what I was doing! I managed to get him to the top but not into his bedroom, he ended up on the on the landing floor, laughing no less.

By now Ella was up and when either one is drunk, the other videos it to remind them of the events! He's a big lad and I was weak and Ella only had one arm, so we couldn't lift him and he wouldn't move. He looked awful, bloodshot eyes and slurred speech; it was only later that I learnt how much he had drunk, on his drinking challenges. He kept babbling and moaning but we had no idea what he was trying to say, after an age we managed to get him to his feet and get him into bed. I was worried in case he was sick, so I tried to put him on his side and I sat there hoping he would nod off but he just kept jabbering on, so after 10 minutes I gave up and went into my room, whilst still listening out. Then the little bugger started playing music on his phone, so I went in and took it off him and threatened to hide it and he said,

"You're like Sedusa."

"What?"

"You know with snakes in your hair!"

"Oh, you mean Medusa?"

"Yyeeesss."

He thought that he was hilarious, it was a bit funny actually but I didn't let him see that, I left him to it and he was happily talking away, mainly to himself, for another 10 minutes before he went quiet. I crept back in to check and he was fast asleep. I couldn't believe that two nights in a row I had been up with my two kids, you never stop being a parent, do you?

The following morning, I had a lie in, until about 10am, then Jacks' friend Jack came around making fun of how drunk Jack had been, I told him that I'd never seen him that drunk. Jack often comes around after a big night out, I do breakfast, which Jack often brings and the kids talk about their night while I listen to their antics! It worries me how drunk youngsters sometimes get now-a-days, I know that me and my mates got drunk but I don't think that it was to that degree, but on the other hand I could have selective memory!

One of Ella's best friends, Katie popped with goodies for Ella, which cheered her up somewhat. Then Tes and Macy arrived to sort out Ella's new bed, normally Ella would have done it but she was incapacitated, I didn't have the energy and Jack is useless at that type of thing. By 1.30 everyone had gone and a relative peace had descended, we had our roast. Then a quick chill before the odious task of helping get Ella ready, she wasn't in the best of moods and apparently, I wasn't helping. Jack was struggling with a hangover, which was what he deserved. What a performance the next morning; first I had a shower, then I had to wash Ella's hair and I was not up to her exacting standard AT ALL! I helped her wash her back and get out but she managed to do the rest herself. I was going out for lunch with my friend Lisa, so I escaped for a few hours, we went to the Peacock which had been refurbished and it was lovely and so was the food. Lisa regaled me with tales of her trip to Edinburgh, I'd been a couple of times but on school trips chaperoning kids and I had loved it. I called for some medication and dressings for Ella's arm, as they couldn't give us any at the hospital. I got home by 3.30am to more drama as Ella was getting ready to go out and getting frustrated because she couldn't dress herself. Both Jack and Ella were meeting their dad and Julie for Julie's birthday lunch, they were going to Nandos, which had recently opened in town. Meanwhile, I was left unloading the Christmas order, it took me forever to do, I had about an hour's quiet time before they were back and chatting away and Ella was in a far better mood.

The following day, I was going to see the new Star Wars film 'Star Wars – the force awakens' with Joanna, I had prepared by watching the other Star Wars films over the weeks, so that I was gemmed up. We loved it; lots of action, some old characters and great new ones too, a fab story line and a well thought out transition from old to new. So, all in all, a huge success, I hate it when you go with big expectations but the film doesn't live up to them, my biggest pet peeve is a bad ending, a bad ending can spoil a good film. Home and I was in for another treat, watching the Downton bafta tribute, it was marvelous, I loved that too.

Macy had more toys and stuff than any child I knew, so I wanted to do something different for her for Christmas, she likes musicals and sings along to the songs from Annie so I booked 'ANNIE the musical' for me and her to go to in the new year. I also printed off the cruise stuff, which I had bought Jack and Ella, as part of their Christmas boxes. Then I was distracted and I spent a good time researching the cruise ship we were going on, it was the Britannia, P and O's newest, largest ship; I was so, so looking forward to going on our cruise, it seemed like we had been waiting for forever. I still needed to sort out my clothes but I had plenty, and if I was short Tes had plenty more that I could borrow. I spent the evening of the 23rd of December, watching IT'S A WONDERFUL LIFE and wrapping presents, it's a bit of a Christmas tradition for me, it puts me in the mood for Christmas while at the same time reminding me what's important in life.

Chapter 22

Christmas and New Year

CHRISTMAS EVE 2015, I didn't get up until gone 10.30 because basically, I didn't have to. Jack was working and Tes popped round with a mountain of presents for Macy to be hidden away, then she wrapped Jack's presents for him in what can only be described as a mad whirlwind of activity. I needed to get a few last-minute bits and Ella wanted some things too, so we went into Nantwich and we somehow managed to get a good parking space, but we had to sit in the car for a while as it was coming down a storm. Nantwich is a lovely town, full of historic buildings, quaint cafés, lovely restaurants and great park areas, at Christmas it is even more beautiful and appealing.

I paid £500 into my bank account in preparation for the cruise, you had cards on board to pay for things and then you were charged at the end, for all that you had purchased, it would be mainly drinks so I was hoping that £500 would be enough! I was treated to lunch by Ella in St Luke's charity shop, I'd not been before but I had heard some good reports and what a fab place it was. The food was delicious, it was a cute little cafe, plus they also sold gorgeous gifts and vintage clothes and knick knacks; with all proceeds going to St Luke's. Ella bought two vintage dresses which were great; one was glittery, the perfect Christmas dress and the other a pretty Summer dress and only £15 each. I got a vintage casserole dish, that says a lot, I have never particularly liked clothes shopping and now I loathed it, so I bought other things instead. We had a brief wander and bought what we needed, Ella wanted to get her grandma, Lyn, something but she couldn't decide, in the end after a bit of brainstorming, she decided on treating Lyn to a theatre visit.

Back home and I decided on a nap; I absolutely love a nap but I still HATED getting up afterwards!! Christmas Eve is Mark's birthday, so I gave the kids a lift out at 6.15pm, to join their dad for his birthday and Christmas drinks. I was feeling mixed emotions after dropping them off – my friends were busy with their families, Kim was with Ant and Tes had arranged to go to see her friend Julian, so I was on my own. This is an excerpt from my diary,

'After seeing so many people out and about I have to say I'm feeling kind of fed up and a bit blue. On one hand, I'm OK to be in but on the other, I'm feeling I'm missing out on stuff. I may well make more plans next year or go away!!'

It's a difficult one and it was at times like that, that I felt lonely, like I wanted someone to be there for me, but I didn't, so I stayed in and wrapped the rest of the pressies and watched something Christmassy on TV. In previous years we have all camped out, at either mine or Tessa's house but this year we were all meeting up in the morning once we were up. The kids arrived home about 1.30, late enough to have had a good time but earlier enough to be up and alright for Christmas morning.

287

CHRISTMAS DAY, we were finally up about 9 and it was 9.30 before Tessa, Kim and Ant arrived, Macy was coming later because she had spent Christmas Eve at her dad's house. We exchanged our presents, a far quicker process than when Macy is unwrapping hers with us, I have to say. I have never gone mad, mad at Christmas but I always try and make sure that Jack and Ella have the same amount of money spent on them and the same amount of presents too. There were some lovely presents and everyone seemed happy with their lot. Then we called my mum and dad in Spain on face time, so that we can see them, but we often just see the top of their heads. I do miss my mum and dad not being here at Christmas, I remember Christmas being busy and now it was all just quieter.

Ella and Jack left to go to their dads for their second Christmas at 12.30 and Kim and Ant went to Ant's new flat for their Christmas lunch. So, Tes and I sat down to roast leg of lamb and all the trimmings, we'd decided on having no starter, I still left nearly half of mine so Charlie was very pleased with the leftovers. I'd manage to catch my knuckle in the grater, it was a small scratch but boy did it sting and continued to throb, it was a wonder Ella hadn't moaned more because hers was 100 times worse; she had adapted very well using just one arm. Tes set off to pick Macy up about 2pm and I tidied up and had a lovely nap. When Tes and Macy arrived back, Kim and Ant came back to see Macy open her presents; Macy began the mammoth task of unwrapping her presents .....it took a good while. She had so much stuff. Kim and Ant got off and Tes and Macy nipped home about 6 to sort out their dogs. We all sat and watched Strictly Christmas, we love strictly and despite having had a nap, I was still in bed for 10.15.

BOXING DAY, I woke about 9am and Tes had managed to bring me in a cup of tea without waking me, so I drank that before I made a move. Tes and Macy had been up a while and so they got off pretty much straight away, I was happy for some peace and quiet, with no interruptions so I could sit down to watch the last ever DOWNTON!! I was very excited. Jack and Ella arrived home, before I had finished watching it, so I paused it while we caught up on how our days had gone, Then, once we had finished talking, I carried on watching, even Ella who never normally watched it got a little emotional. I loved Downton; the costumes, the settings the story lines and all the references to historical events; in my eyes, it was just perfect and I have the box set so I can watch whenever I want. 'Before' (being ill) Boxing day was a boozy affair for me because the kids always went to their dad's house for a party, it used to be a skoolies night but now not so much and definitely not for me. What we did was to go out early doors; I picked up Joanna and Tes and we went to the Cat and had wines and cocktails and we all got quite merry, putting the world to rights. We needed food so we had a few chips to help soak up the alcohol; we were ready to go home by 7.30 but Jack who was giving us a lift back, didn't finish his gig until nearly 8.30, so, we had another drink to fill the time.

Once we got home, Ella and her gang were getting ready to go out and having a drink as they did, I made myself a cup of tea. Ella was a bit cautious about getting her arm knocked when she was out but it didn't stop her going, she just had a bandage on so that people could see to be careful around her. They all left about 10 and I was in bed straight after. At 2.45am the phone rang, I hate it when it does when the kids are out; it was Ella, she said that one of her friends wasn't feeling well and she was on her way back here, could I keep an eye on her until she herself got home? She was with another friend whose boyfriend had gotten into trouble, Ella arrived about half an hour later and took over duties. She definitely has a gift for looking after people. The next day I was up by 10.30, Becky had stayed over and Jack's friend Jack T, arrived feeling crappy it was like counsellor central, most weeks. So, drinks and food were supplied to the troops, then Ella's friend Nikki arrived and wasn't in the best mood because of her boyfriend; listening to them all it was funny, replaying what they had been doing the night before. Jack T comes that often, after having a drink, that he often brings supplies with him; bacon, eggs, meat, flowers even!

Later I had some nibbles whilst watching SOUTHPAW, which Jack had bought me for Christmas, plus the kids ordered food in which saved me cooking. I was feeling a bit off, I was fine lying down but each time I stood up I was feeling dodgy, sickie and dizzy too, I thought well that's my hangover then! Then I made a brew and I couldn't hold it in my right hand because I'd gotten the shakes; the cup shakes and tea goes everywhere, I get it on a regular basis and it affects my writing too, I hadn't noticed any sort of pattern with it though. By 8 I had pain in my hands and feet especially, I took some tablets and thankfully by bedtime it had eased; I'd begun waking with pins and needles in my hands as well, which was a new one.

The following morning it was 11 before I moved from my bed. Then me, well the kids mainly, blitz cleaned downstairs, it did look so much better but it knackers me out even though I had done very little, I hadn't like cleaning much 'before' but now I hated it. Tes gave me a lift to get my car and on my way back I called to cancel having a paper delivered, for whilst I was travelling. Most things on my to do list had some connection to us travelling, we were on countdown to our cruise already and then we only had two weeks at home before Ella and I were off traveling again on our first adventure to Spain. One big thing which I had yet to sort, was to buy an electric bike, I'd seen a few but they were more than I wanted to spend so I just kept looking. I had a laptop which I would take away in the van, so that I could do some work on SUNSHINE in between sight-seeing, sunbathing and travelling.

I had been reducing my pain medication because I had been on it too long and it could become addictive and I had managed about a week and a half with-out having a Fentanyl patch on but the latest aches and pains had forced me to put half of one, on again, but I woke the next morning and realised that my patch had fallen off anyway! I was feeling a bit washed out as well, so I took an extra steroid hoping it would help me, truth be told I often felt bad after a few busy days; someone left a comment on reviews for my book 'You are my sunshine',

'Anna Gray frustrated me at times. One page she can't get out of bed, the next she's on holiday around Europe.'

I got what she meant to a degree, it did look like one day I was enjoying life, the next I was in bed, but people don't see me behind closed doors; they don't see me spending hours in bed and endless hours in pain, they don't notice that when I stand I often wince in pain, when I am dancing to my favorite song it's only my hands which move, they don't see all the extra medication that I take to get through all of those outings. My feeling is and always has been work hard, play hard; what is life worth, if you don't make memories? I could quite easily stay in bed each day and I probably wouldn't be in quite so much pain, however, I wouldn't have things to look forward to and I wouldn't have a purpose or reason to keep fighting on; so surely that's no sort of life for anyone? Everyone has their opinion but only each of us knows our own truth.

In the afternoon, I took Ella to have her stitches out at the doctor's surgery, she was booked in to see the nurse. The nurse peeled back the dressings and began removing all of the many sterile strips, but when she removed the stitches on her biggest cut on her elbow, the cut came open about ¼ of an inch. Basically, I think that as it was so deep and wide they'd had to do them tight, which meant that the sides were pushed under a bit, so now there's a channel rather than skin meeting. The nurse called the doctor in to have a look and he agreed that it needed to be sterile striped it again, in the hope it would heal a little neater. The other cuts looked neat enough, although she was going to have some significant scars, but she didn't seem too bothered; I worried that it would make her cover her arm and be conscious of it but it didn't.

When we got back and I had a sleep hoping to feel better, because I had plans with the book club to go out for a meal, but when I woke I somehow felt worse, really dizzy and worse so, on standing.

I was feeling dizzy so I thought that I'd have a nap in the hope that I would wake feeling better and I did but the dizziness hadn't gone. I really wasn't sure whether I should go out, especially as I'd volunteered to drive to pick up Tor. So, I had some milk and more steroids and I felt a tad better; I didn't want to let people down, so I rallied and got ready. I picked Tor and Elaine up and we met Deb and Joanna there, once I was settled I began to feel better. We had a lovely meal and most of the conversation, was about counting our lucky stars after Tor had had a bad car accident, then there was Ella's and other people who had had a bad Christmas, who we knew. We didn't leave until 10.15, I hadn't drunk, so I was taxi for the night. I went to bed keeping my fingers crossed, that I would feel better the next day, I just felt that something was off!

I woke still feeling dizzy and I was a bit baffled as to why. Ella got up and was all restless and suffering from cabin fever bless her, she likes being busy, she is happy to have slobby days but she needed plenty of experiences and outings to get her through; but as the weather was so rubbish we were a little restricted. We did consider the cinema but there was nothing on that we fancied, after an age we decided on going out for lunch. Ella drove with some difficulty with a straight left arm doing the gears, we were going to Ella's favorite pub, 'The pheasant inn', when we arrived the car park was jammed but we managed to squeeze in. It is always, busy,

busy and the food was always gorgeous; I just had ham, egg and chips but thick slabs of ham and Ella had a big portion of fish and chips. We were too full for puds! We went home and watched MAGIC MIKE XXL, but we found it very odd, uncomfortable viewing ,there was a lot going on, all I can say is, no wonder it was called XXL!

New Year's Eve, I was up by 9.15 encouraged by a delivery of some clothes for me!! I tried on the clothes I had ordered; the bikini was a little small but I gave it a good stretch, so I was hoping that it would be ok, the other pieces fit me ok so they went in my 'cruise' pile. I had a nap and woke still feeling somewhat dizzy, I had a shower and I got ready, slowly, for my night out. I am not a big lover of New Year, when I was younger and when I was married I seemed to enjoy it but as I've gotten older it has always been a bit of an anti-climax, maybe I need to do something wildly different, or go away or maybe find a man to share it with? I had not even thought about having a man in my life, there was too much going on and in 2016 there was even more happening; if things went to plan then I would be away for about half the year so that wouldn't be ideal for a relationship, would it?

Once I was ready, I gave Jack and his friend Taylor a lift out to the Boot pub, in Nantwich. Ella had gone off to Dublin with her step-sister Katie, lucky girl! Then I joined Tessa and Joanna at Willaston club, it was just around the corner for both of them, so it was easy and convenient and there was a fantastic Elvis tribute on. It was busy and Paul, the Elvis tribute, came on after 9pm but it was so loud, I was developing a bad head. Tes had brought along some cheese and biscuits for us and in the break of the show we helped ourselves. When Paul came back on after the break and the music started up again, it was just as loud and my head was getting worse, so at 10.40 I'd had enough, I was happy to go home. I made a brew and I was going to go to sleep but I didn't want to start the New Year asleep, so I stayed awake until after 12 and saw the New Year in and I watched the fireworks on the telly and outside too, they were fantastic.

New Year has traditionally been a time when people make resolutions; to set themselves goals to achieve, to lose weight, to stop drinking, to eat more healthily. For me my resolutions went back to when I was in hospital after my operation, I hadn't been able to sleep and I had some sort of epiphany or something, in the end I turned on my light and wrote a list of what I wanted to do with my money, this was my list;

- A cruise, with the kids
- Do my drive and garage at home
- Newer car
- Motorhome
- Extension?
- Travel month by month
- Tes take on a Spa retreat
- Take mum and dad somewhere
- Treat Book club to a weekend away
- Take other friends out for meals etc.
- Write a book...........

So I had ticked off a few but I still had some to complete. I had felt like 2015 was about me being ill, getting radiation, recovering, having tests and appointments, sleeping! And for me it wasn't the focus that I wanted to have in my life, I wanted to look forward. Statistics showed that there was a significant chance that my tumour would grow again and I may not be so lucky next time; I may be left even more damaged by an operation, or maybe they wouldn't be able to operate. I was living my life as much as I could and if it didn't grow again then I would continue to do, as much as I could and if it did grow, then I will have least I will have lived some and followed my dreams.

2015 had been a good year too, if you ignored the health bits; I'd had some amazing holidays, I'd spent more time with the people I loved, I'd reconnected to people who I'd lost contact with, I'd been to new places, I'd had lots of fun. I was very grateful for those moments and for all the people who made them so special; in life, we can all have curve balls thrown in our direction but sometimes it can be like a beacon of light to show us where we should be going and what we should be focusing on. I am so grateful for my wonderful children, for my brilliant group of friends and for my fantastic family; it takes a bit of team effort, when the going gets tough and I had the best team ever. So, looking to the future, I was taking back control, I would be taking as many holidays as I could, I would be going out to the theatre, I would be doing as much as my body would allow and then some. All of my experiences had shown me that being positive and focused on something good, helps your mind and body in so many ways. Having a good support system of loved ones, as the advert says 'is priceless!' It was important for me to shift my focus and along with it other people's focus too, 2016 was going to be an amazing year for me; I would visit places which I had never visited, I would have once in a lifetime holidays, I would be living, not just surviving......

If you want to see some pictures and put faces to names mentioned in the book then check out my Facebook page -
https://www.facebook.com/annagrayauthor

Plus I have a new blog site
https://agray666999.wixsite.com/mysite

please check it out and leave a comment!

I hope very much that you enjoyed this book, if you did, then I would be truly grateful, if you could please leave a review on Amazon for me.

Also look out for the third instalment of my story, **'I want to live, not just survive',** which will be as much about my travelling experiences as my health struggles.

Much love Anna Gray xxx

21134752R00170

Printed in Poland
by Amazon Fulfillment
Poland Sp. z o.o., Wrocław